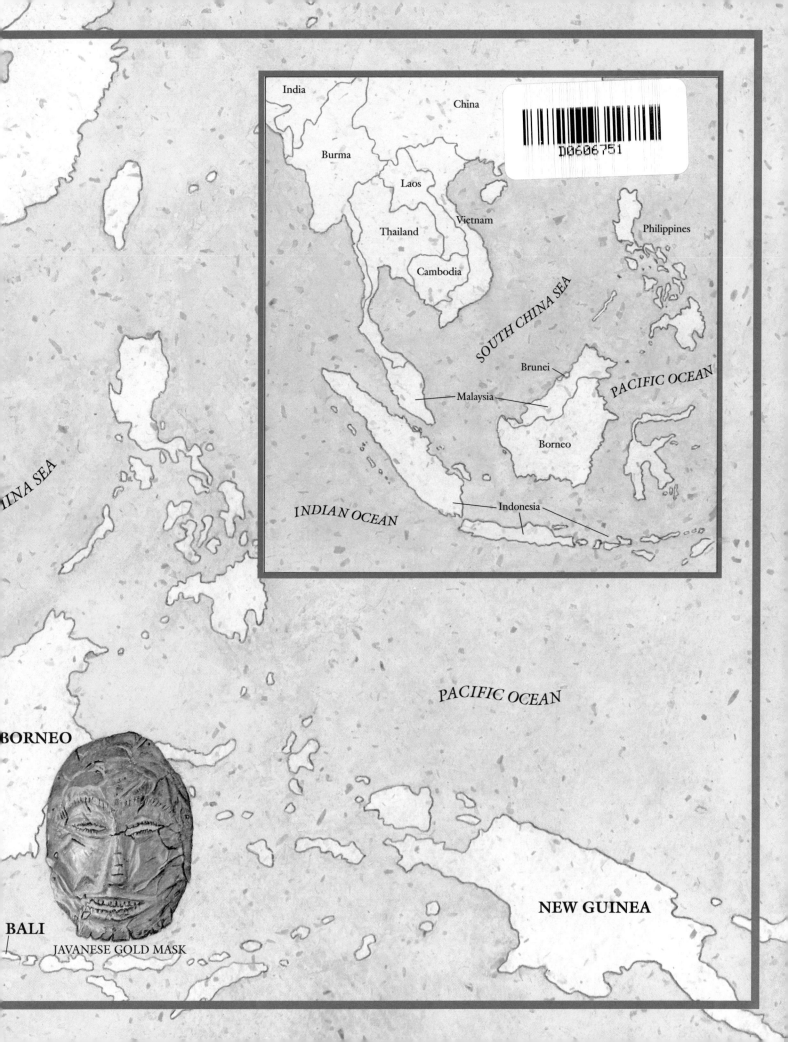

India

China

Burma

Laos

Vietnam

Thailand

Cambodia

SOUTH CHINA SEA

Philippines

Brunei

PACIFIC OCEAN

Malaysia

Borneo

INDIAN OCEAN

Indonesia

PACIFIC OCEAN

CHINA SEA

BORNEO

NEW GUINEA

BALI

JAVANESE GOLD MASK

TIME® LIFE BOOKS

Other Publications:

THE TIME-LIFE COMPLETE
 GARDENER
THE NEW HOME REPAIR AND
 IMPROVEMENT
JOURNEY THROUGH THE MIND
 AND BODY
WEIGHT WATCHERS® SMART CHOICE
 RECIPE COLLECTION
TRUE CRIME
THE AMERICAN INDIANS
THE ART OF WOODWORKING
ECHOES OF GLORY
THE NEW FACE OF WAR
HOW THINGS WORK
WINGS OF WAR
CREATIVE EVERYDAY COOKING
COLLECTOR'S LIBRARY OF THE
 UNKNOWN
CLASSICS OF WORLD WAR II
TIME-LIFE LIBRARY OF CURIOUS AND
 UNUSUAL FACTS
AMERICAN COUNTRY
VOYAGE THROUGH THE UNIVERSE
THE THIRD REICH
MYSTERIES OF THE UNKNOWN
TIME FRAME
FIX IT YOURSELF
FITNESS, HEALTH & NUTRITION
SUCCESSFUL PARENTING
HEALTHY HOME COOKING
UNDERSTANDING COMPUTERS
LIBRARY OF NATIONS
THE ENCHANTED WORLD
THE KODAK LIBRARY OF CREATIVE
 PHOTOGRAPHY
GREAT MEALS IN MINUTES
THE CIVIL WAR
PLANET EARTH
COLLECTOR'S LIBRARY OF THE CIVIL
 WAR
THE EPIC OF FLIGHT
THE GOOD COOK
WORLD WAR II
THE OLD WEST

*For information on and a full description of
any of the Time-Life Books series listed above,
please call 1-800-621-7026 or write:*
Reader Information
Time-Life Customer Service
P.O. Box C-32068
Richmond, Virginia 23261-2068

Cover: Found in 1927 by a farmer on the island of Java, this exquisitely crafted head of a Bodhisattva, an enlightened disciple of Buddha, is made of solid silver. The statue to which it belongs dates to the early 10th century AD and is a reflection of the religious and artistic culture of India that, when merged with native traditions throughout Southeast Asia, inspired local artisans to produce works of outstanding beauty. The elaborately carved stone floral pattern that is used here as a background decorates a temple in the ancient religious complex of Angkor in modern Cambodia and is characteristic of the Khmer bas-reliefs covering many of the structures there.

End paper: The important archaeological sites, cities, islands, and major rivers that make up the area known as Southeast Asia are located on this end-paper map painted by Paul Breeden. The icons represent various cultures that existed in the region from 8000 BC to AD 1400. Modern political boundaries are drawn on the inset map. Breeden also painted the images illustrating the timeline on pages 158-159.

SOUTHEAST ASIA:
A PAST
REGAINED

Time-Life Books is a division of Time Life
  Inc.

PRESIDENT and CEO: John M. Fahey Jr.

TIME-LIFE BOOKS

MANAGING EDITOR: Roberta Conlan

Director of Design: Michael Hentges
Editorial Production Manager: Ellen Robling
Senior Editors: Russell B. Adams Jr., Dale M.
  Brown, Janet Cave, Lee Hassig, Robert
  Somerville, Henry Woodhead
Special Projects Editor: Rita Thievon Mullin
Director of Operations: Eileen Bradley
Director of Photography and Research: John
  Conrad Weiser
Library: Louise D. Forstall

PRESIDENT: John D. Hall

*Vice President, Director of New Product
  Development:* Neil Kagan
Vice President, Book Production: Marjann
  Caldwell
Production Manager: Marlene Zack
Quality Assurance Manager: James King

**Library of Congress
Cataloging in Publication Data**
  Southeast Asia: a past regained / by the edi-
tors of Time-Life Books.
    p. cm.   —(Lost civilizations)
  Includes bibliographical references (p.   )
and index.
  ISBN 0-8094-9112-5
    1. Asia, Southeastern—Civilization.
    2. Asia, Southeastern—Antiquities.
  I. Time-Life Books. II. Series.
  DS523.2.S68   1995
  959'.01—dc20   95-34501
                                        CIP

R 10 9 8 7 6 5 4 3 2 1

LOST CIVILIZATIONS

SERIES EDITOR: Dale M. Brown

Administrative Editor: Philip Brandt George

Editorial staff for *Southeast Asia: A Past
  Regained*
Art Director: Bill McKenney
Picture Editor: Marion Ferguson Briggs
Text Editors: Russell B. Adams Jr. (principal),
  Charlotte Anker, Robin Currie, Charles J.
  Hagner
Associate Editors/Research-Writing: Katherine
  L. Griffin, Mary Grace Mayberry,
  Jacqueline L. Shaffer, Jarelle S. Stein
Senior Copyeditor: Barbara Fairchild Quarmby
Picture Coordinator: Catherine Parrott
Editorial Assistant: Patricia D. Whiteford
Special Contributors: Anthony Allan, Timothy
  Cooke, Thomas Lewis (text); Arlene
  Borden, Ann-Louise G. Gates, Ylann
  Schemm, Barry N. Wolverton (research);
  Roy Nanovic (index).

Correspondents: Christine Hinze (London),
Christina Lieberman (New York), Maria Vin-
cenza Aloisi (Paris). Valuable assistance was
also provided by: Grant Peck (Bangkok); For-
rest Anderson (Beijing); Elizabeth Kraemer-
Singh, Angelica Lemmer (Bonn); Barbara
Gevene Hertz (Copenhagen); Frank Gibney
(Hanoi); William Dowell (Hong Kong); Bam-
bang Harymurti, Michael Shari (Jakarta);
Judy Aspinall (London); John Dunne (Mel-
bourne); Saskia Van de Linde (The Netherlands); Meenakshi Ganguly (New Delhi);
Elizabeth Brown, Suzanne Davis (New York);
Ann Natanson (Rome); Ellen White (Singapore); Dick Berry (Tokyo).

The Consultants:

Joyce C. White, research specialist at the University of Pennsylvania Museum, is director of
the archaeological project at Ban Chiang,
Thailand, and was guest curator for a Smithsonian Institution traveling exhibition of the
Ban Chiang finds. The author of numerous articles and scholarly papers, White concentrates
on Southeast Asian archaeology, with special
emphasis on the emergence of agriculture and
the development of social complexity.

John N. Miksic has taught archaeology at
two Indonesian universities and is currently
senior lecturer in the Department of History
and the Southeast Asian Studies Program
at the National University of Singapore. He
conducts annual excavations in East Java
and is the author of three books, including
Ancient Javanese Gold and *Borobudur: Golden
Tales of the Buddhas.*

Robert L. Brown is associate professor of Indian and Southeast Asian art history at the
University of California at Los Angeles and
serves as adjunct curator of Southeast Asian
art at the Pacific Asia Museum in Pasadena.
His particular area of interest is the relationship between Indian influences and early
Southeast Asian art, culture, and religion. He
is the author of numerous publications.

This volume is one in a series that explores
the worlds of the past, using the finds of archaeologists and other scientists to bring ancient peoples and their cultures vividly to life.

Other volumes in the series include:

SOUTHEAST ASIA: A PAST REGAINED

By the Editors of Time-Life Books

TIME-LIFE BOOKS, ALEXANDRIA, VIRGINIA

CONTENTS

Algae-tinted stones like these of the Ta Prohm temple at Angkor in Cambodia capture the elegiac mood of Southeast Asia's abandoned, jungle-overgrown cities. A 19th-century French explorer-artist who visited Angkor mused: "Sad fragility of human things! What riches and treasures of art will remain forever buried beneath these ruins; how many distinguished men—artists, sovereigns, and warriors—are now forgotten!

SURPRISES HIDDEN IN THE JUNGLE

Characteristic swirling lines decorate this 2,000-year-old pot (inset) from Ban Chiang, Thailand. Excavations there in the 1970s (background) seemed to indicate the existence of a prehistoric, Southeast Asian culture far more sophisticated than anyone had dreamed.

While walking through the village of Ban Chiang in northeastern Thailand in 1966, Stephen Young tripped on the root of a kapok tree, fell headlong, and launched one of the major archaeological discoveries of the 20th century. Young— a third-year college student and son of a former U. S. ambassador to Thailand—had been doing sociological research in the area when, because of his encounter with the root, he suddenly found himself studying a small patch of ground at extremely close range. It was then that he noticed a ceramic ring protruding from the soil. On closer inspection, it turned out to be the rim of a partially buried clay pot. Nearby there were another, another, and another—a profusion of pottery, long buried in the earth, most of it broken into pieces that were now being slowly exposed by erosion. They were buff in color, painted with striking, bold designs in crimson. And Young noticed that the sherds were not glazed, and so must have been very old.

Young pocketed a few pieces of the pottery and, on his return to Bangkok, showed them to some experts. Among them was Elizabeth Lyons, a consultant to the U.S. State Department. She recalled having seen some similar pottery fragments—possibly from the same village—six years earlier. At the time, she recalled, "the Thais had little interest in the prehistoric, or pre-Buddhist period, and had no experience with the special demands of a prehistoric excavation."

But all of that had changed by 1967. Reminded of the unusual pottery to be found in Ban Chiang, the Thai government's Fine Arts Department made an exploratory excavation in the village. When the diggers found stone tools and—most intriguing—small bronze artifacts among the pottery, Lyons recalled, "we realized it was most probably important." Samples of the pottery were sent to the Applied Science Center for Archaeology at the University of Pennsylvania Museum of Archaeology and Anthropology. There, a team had just completed tests of a new technique for dating fired earthenware by exposing it to high temperatures and measuring the thermoluminescence, or faint light, emitted by the discharge of radioactive energy from elements in the clay. Because this energy seemed to accumulate at a predictable rate, and the original firing would have released all of it and reset the "atomic clock" to zero, it appeared possible to accurately gauge when a piece of pottery was made. Tantalizingly, tests of the Ban Chiang material indicated that some of the pottery was over 6,000 years old.

American archaeologist Wilhelm G. Solheim II carefully pieces together a third-millennium-BC clay jar from the Thai site of Non Nok Tha. An innovative thinker, Solheim pioneered some of the first systematic excavations of prehistoric sites in Thailand during the 1960s.

"My first reaction was to disbelieve," recalled Froelich Rainey, then director of the University Museum. No Bronze Age site of such antiquity had ever been found, or suspected, in Southeast Asia or elsewhere. Indeed, the dawn of the classic Bronze Age in Mesopotamia is dated about 3000 BC. Isolated finds in Eastern Europe and the greater Mesopotamia region dating to the fourth millennium BC are thought to indicate where metalsmiths first discovered that tin alloyed with copper made a stronger, more workable metal.

News of the thermoluminescence dating reached Thailand in 1969 and set off a frenzy of private digging, selling, and collecting that crescendoed in early 1972. Villagers harvested a cash crop of ancient pottery that was snapped up by collectors, many of them U.S. Air Force personnel from the base at nearby Udorn. In July 1972, when the Thai government banned private trading in Ban Chiang artifacts and required registration of those already removed, 8,000 pots were registered. No one knows how many went unrecorded.

Thai government archaeologists had found that the village of Ban Chiang was located on an ancient cemetery containing thousands of graves. Overwhelmed by the volume of the material—tools and adornments of stone, bronze, and iron, as well as at least four distinct types of pottery—they formed a partnership with the University Museum and began one of the most important excavations in the history of Southeast Asian archaeology, and one with profound implications for an understanding of how civilizations develop.

Until the mid-1960s, Southeast Asia had been seen as a backwater of history, into which occasional eddies of progress had swirled from the more advanced cultures of India, China, or possibly even Eastern Europe. Thereafter, however, with the newest technology and best methods of archaeology brought to bear on such finds as the one stumbled on by Stephen Young, the world would be forced to change its thinking about the region. In the words of Wilhelm G. Solheim II, an early leader of this reformation and now retired from the University of Hawaii, field research in Southeast Asia would encounter a sudden profusion of "astonishing discoveries about the ancient history and prehistory of the people who live there."

Solheim and others would eventually find evidence that greater Southeast Asia may have witnessed some of the world's earliest agriculture, produced some of its earlier metalworking, and stimulated one of the largest diasporas in the history of humankind—that of the so-called Austronesian (from the Greek *austro,* or "southern," and the Latin *nesis,* or "island") speakers. Carrying with them their common family of languages, these hardy seafarers ranged halfway around the globe to Madagascar and Easter Island. These revelations would have a profound effect on historical thought. "Even the position of Western man and his place in the evolution of world culture may be drastically affected," wrote Solheim. "For clear and powerful indications are emerging that some of the earliest steps toward civilization may have been taken in Southeast Asia."

Southeast Asia was once a subcontinent-sized peninsula jutting toward Australia from China, dwarfing India. At the end of the Ice Age, about 10,000 years ago, the area was infiltrated by rising seawater. Its central lowlands became the floor of the shallow South China Sea, and its loftiest southern promontories and ridges became the great archipelago known today as Indonesia. A portion of this arc of islands, from Sumatra eastward past Java and Bali, is one of the most violently active volcanic regions on earth. Mainland Southeast Asia is made up of the present-day countries of Myanmar (Burma), Thailand, Laos, Cambodia, Vietnam, and the Malay Peninsula of Malaysia. Culturally, that portion of modern-day China that lies south of the Yangzi (Yangtze) River is also considered to have been a part of Southeast Asia in ancient times.

The elevation of the mainland rises steadily from the tropical and sea-level south to the mountainous and subtropical north. The mountains along the northern rim of Southeast Asia, namely the eastern Himalayan foothills, are pierced by great rivers flowing southward from the highlands of Tibet toward the South China Sea, among them the Salween, Mekong, and Yangzi. Two north-south mountain chains partition the region: one, the Annam Cordillera, walls off the valley of the Mekong from the South China Sea to the east; and a series of ridges west of the Mekong extend southward far enough to form the backbone of the Malay Peninsula.

As the civilizations of mainland Southeast Asia were partitioned by mountains, they were connected and defined by the great rivers that provided arteries of travel, communication, and trade. The Yangzi separated the region geographically, if not culturally, from China. The Mekong flows out of southwest China, forming much of the present-day boundary between Laos and Thailand, then traverses eastern Cambodia and spreads its huge delta across southernmost Vietnam. Along with Thailand's Chao Phraya, Burma's Salween and Irrawaddy, and Vietnam's Red, or Hong, these rivers with their alluvial valleys also provided the region's richest agricultural soils by laying down layers of silt year after year during seasonal flooding.

The region's many islands were defined by the surrounding water and by their proximity to the mainland and to one another. The island climate is largely equatorial, with heavy rains falling throughout the year. Most of the mainland, however, is subtropical, with a dry season for half the year. Each year from May to September the seasonal southwest monsoon brings saturating rains to most of the area, swelling the rivers to flood stage and quadrupling the area

As in the past, Vietnamese river craft bearing rice, vegetables, fish, and meat travel the Mekong toward floating markets. Formed by the congregation of several boats with goods for sale, such markets seem a natural development in Southeast Asia, where waterways run like highways throughout the region and historically served for the transmission not only of goods but also of cultural influences.

of Cambodia's Tonle Sap, or "Great Lake." The flow is so great that the Tonle Sap River, one of the lower tributaries of the great Mekong, cannot discharge it and begins running backward into the lake.

Europeans became involved in the region as they searched for aromatic spices and began to establish trading outposts on the islands of the so-called East Indies during the 16th century. The Portuguese led the incursion, and they began the fabulously profitable East India trade in such seasonings as nutmeg, cloves, and mace. Portugal enjoyed a virtual monopoly in the spice trade until the beginning of the 17th century, when England and Holland used their superior naval strength to drive Portugal away from most of its outposts.

As trade expanded—from spices to such other raw materials as rubber, tea, and tin—and became more competitive, a succession of countries used military power to colonize the sources of trade. While England was preoccupied with India—and later, Burma—France and Holland moved into Southeast Asia. The Dutch secured Java, Sumatra, and the so-called Spice Islands firmly enough to retain their grip on the spice trade well into the 20th century. The French gravitated to mainland Southeast Asia, and in the second half of the 19th century, they established their hegemony over what is known today as southern Vietnam (then called Cochin China). They next took over the northern Vietnamese provinces of Annam and Tonkin, then Cambodia and Laos. The French combined all these territories and their peoples into a colony they called Indochina, a name implying that in their judgment the region was a mere geographical and cultural appendage of its giant continental neighbors. The only part of the region to retain its independence through the entire colonial period was the country known before World War II as Siam and today as Thailand.

The Europeans who came to the area during these centuries were not particularly interested in the culture or history of the aborigines. One exception was French emissary Simon dè la Loubere, who in 1687 negotiated a commercial treaty with the king of Siam. Unlike most colonialists, dè la Loubere took note of the people he met and was perplexed by them. "It would be difficult to judge," he wrote, whether the Siamese "are a single people, directly descended from the first men that inhabited the country of Siam, or whether in the process of time some other nation has not also settled there, notwithstanding the first inhabitants." It was an intriguing question, but one that would not be addressed by scholars for centuries.

In 1858, as the French were beginning to extend their influence throughout the region, a scholar named Henri Mouhot undertook a voyage of scientific investigation—the first by a European into mainland Southeast Asia. His journals, published posthumously in 1864, drew attention to such archaeological treasures as the great monuments of Angkor, north of Cambodia's Tonle Sap. Forgotten for centuries and overgrown by the jungle, these sprawling temple complexes—elaborately ornamented and filled with intriguing sculpture and enigmatic inscriptions—bespoke a wealthy and advanced civilization whose presence had been previously unsuspected by Europeans. Mouhot made no effort to interpret what he saw, merely sketching, describing, and moving on. Of the Angkor inscriptions he wrote that "until some learned archaeologist shall devote himself to the subject," only "contradictory speculations will be promulgated."

It took four decades for interest in these monumental ruins to rise to the level of organized action, but in 1898 the French colonial authorities founded the École Française d'Extrême Orient (EFEO). This tax-supported academy for Southeast Asian studies established a library, a museum, and a permanent archaeological mission that had access to all the known ruins in Indochina. With that access, of course, went the power of decision over proposals to explore and study them. As a result, French scholars for years carried out most of the investigations of Indochina's ancient civilizations.

The French École began to document and interpret an earlier period of foreign cultural infiltration that bore some resemblance to their own—the spread of Indian culture across the region during the first millennium AD. Like the French in the 19th century, the Indians of about two millennia before had arrived as traders and set up outposts along the coasts. Apparently, the indigenous inhabitants were attracted to the culture brought by the Indians, and Indian economic and religious influence extended throughout the region. They found great wealth there, along with great opportunities for the spread of their Hindu and Buddhist religions.

Archaeological expeditions of increasing frequency and size not only learned more about Angkor—identifying it as the capital of a powerful Khmer empire of the late first millennium AD—but also discovered other great Khmer cities long buried by the Cambodian jungles. Moreover, they came across evidence of a similar but separate civilization, the Cham, that had existed about the same time in central and southern coastal Vietnam. The inscriptions, in both Sanskrit—the language of ancient India—and the local vernacular (either Khmer or Cham, depending on the region), turned out to be historical and financial records from which it was possible to sketch a history of the two empires, dating back to what the French assumed was the empires' sudden appearance in Southeast Asia.

From archaeological evidence, the French scholars learned a little about the indigenous peoples encountered by the arriving Indians: that they lived in villages and sometimes walled towns of thatched wood-and-bamboo houses raised on pilings. It was also apparent that similar cultures, as expressed in the form of their houses, animist beliefs, funeral customs, and agricultural practices, existed for some time across mainland Indochina, Sumatra, Borneo, New Guinea, and the islands of Micronesia and Polynesia. The scholars were also aware that certain elements of the Khmer and Cham cultures were distinctly non-Indian—the emphasis on placating the spirits of the countryside and the dead, for example, and in the importance of certain ceremonial utensils, such as bronze drums and stones. But the French were scarcely more interested in the ancient indigenous culture than they were in the natives of their own time.

One of the prominent investigators was Georges Coedès, a director of the École, who from the 1920s to the 1950s translated and interpreted all the Sanskrit inscriptions to be found at the time on the monuments of Indochina. In addition to establishing the basic outlines for the history of the dynasties that had produced the monuments, Coedès and others tried to place them in a wider context. Coedès believed, as did most scholars of his time, that civilization had radiated outward from Mesopotamia to Egypt, then Athens, then Rome. The age of the great monuments and imperial cities of India and China indicated that they had been next. As this wave of civilization spread, he felt, it eventually washed over Southeast Asia.

In Coedès's view it must have happened just like the colonization with which he was familiar: Advanced people must have bestowed the gifts of civilization upon ignorant and grateful aborigines. The Indian benefactors—he referred to the entire region as "Farther India"—encountered recipients who, Coedès wrote in 1966, "seem to have been lacking in creative genius and showed little aptitude for making progress without stimulus from the outside."

British historian Grahame Clark said as late as 1971 that the prehistoric people of Southeast Asia had never progressed from the Stone Age into the age of metals, as other cultures had moved from Copper through Bronze to Iron Ages. Clark wrote that, unlike Mesopotamia and China for example, in Southeast Asia, "stone tools continued in general use into the Christian era." Although the first prehistoric site found in the region, noted in 1879, had included some bronze implements in its large mound of potsherds and shells, Clark and others dismissed such evidence as anomalous. Perhaps a few items of bronze

gist Russell Ciochon and archaeologist John Olsen to Vietnam in 1989. Their reason for probing Vietnam was sound: Southern China, where most of the known *Gigantopithecus* fossils had been found, was picked over, both by archaeologists and by Asian pharmacists who sought fossils to use in the preparations of age-old medicines. Vietnam, where Giganto remains had also been found, was comparatively virgin territory. For Americans, though, the country was taboo. In the late 1980s one could not even phone Vietnam from the United States, much less fly directly to Hanoi. So Ciochon had to resort to cloak-and-dagger methods: While working in Thailand he got in touch with the Vietnamese embassy in Bangkok through a contact at the American embassy there. Shortly after, Ciochon and Olsen found themselves part of the first American team ever to participate jointly in the field with Vietnamese scientists.

The team dug for two weeks in the Lang Trang Caves, which an initial survey showed to be fossil rich. While Ciochon and Olsen did not find any new Giganto bones, they did find hundreds of relics that helped flesh out the environment in which Giganto and *Homo erectus* coexisted for 500,000 years. They also created a lasting relationship with the Vietnamese, culminating in a visit to the United States in 1990 by two Vietnamese scientists.

Using a state-of-the-art German rock saw, Ciochon removes chunks of fossil-flecked material from the Lang Trang Caves in Vietnam. In the end, his team recovered more than 1,000 fossils representing 36 different mammalian species.

John Olsen (below, on the left) *and Nguyen Van Binh examine a fossil they have found in the floor of Cave Four. Buried in this spot was a Bronze Age hearth—recognizable because the earth was dark and hard from continual fire making—and the teeth of a pig, cow, porcupine, and deer, perhaps remnants of an ancient meal.*

Prehistoric hunter-gatherers made these three flaked-stone tools, which are characteristic of a stone-tool technology named Hoabinhian after the Vietnamese site where it was first identified. American archaeologist Chester Gorman discovered the artifacts (probably used for a variety of tasks) in northwest Thailand's Spirit Cave during the mid-1960s.

and iron from other cultures, he wrote, had found their way into northern Vietnam to be deposited "in the richer graves of Annam."

To be sure, not all French archaeology had focused on the relics of great civilizations, and not all investigators ignored the increasing incidence of anomalies in the prehistoric record. In the 1920s, for example, Madeleine Colani began investigating coastal sites showing evidence of Stone Age inhabitation.

Colani's efforts were supported not by the French École but by the Geological Service of the Indochinese Union. A botanist who had become a paleontologist and then an archaeologist, Colani was working in the Vietnamese province of Hoa Binh, across the Red River Delta from Hanoi. There, she studied the remains of hunter-gatherers found in rock shelters or caves where traces of ancient foodstuffs, mostly animal bones, had been preserved under the roofs.

Colani identified a distinctive hunter-gatherer culture, which she called Hoabinhian, that had flourished after the extinction of the megafauna—huge creatures such as mammoths, giant ground sloths, and saber-toothed cats—at the end of the Ice Age. Evidence of Hoabinhian stone-tool users would later be found over most of Southeast Asia, from south China to the Malay Peninsula and west to Burma—a geographic dispersal that led scholars to conclude that Hoabinhian remains were not those of a single people but rather of a widespread stone-tool technology.

At first, Colani's findings seemed to confirm the traditional view of the native people as lagging behind the rest of the world. The distinctive tool of the Hoabinhian culture was a rounded river cobble, later called a sumatralith, that was flaked around one side. The seeming crudity of this implement—its coarse flaking and lack of retouch or finish—was taken as evidence that the people who made it were somewhat backward compared with their contemporaries and even predecessors in Europe, who had long been producing finely flaked implements. On the other hand, Colani and subsequent researchers of the Hoabinhian culture were puzzled to find pottery in its later deposits, seeming to date to 8,000 years ago—long before the inhabitants of Southeast Asia supposedly learned to make pottery.

Even more perplexing were the recurrent discoveries at Dong Son, in northern Vietnam, of large, decorative bronze drums *(pages 48 and 50)* that indicated a highly developed prehistoric metallurgy. This required another, even more complex explanation of how, yet again, the natives had been brought unexpected gifts from afar. And in 1932 the Austrian anthropologist Robert Heine-Geldern proposed a scenario that would become the paradigm for interpreting any such anomalies in Southeast Asian prehistory. Confronted with the appearance at several sites of an advanced, rectangular stone adze not consistent with the more primitive and familiar river cobbles, Heine-Geldern proposed that the area had experienced "waves of culture," a succession of migrations bringing advanced techniques into Southeast Asia. The adze people, he proposed, must have come from northern China. To account for the bronze metallurgy at Dong Son, Heine-Geldern simply hypothesized another wave, this one of an advanced people from Eastern Europe who moved southeastward about 1000 BC and arrived in Southeast Asia 500 years later.

Despite the lack of supporting archaeological evidence, this hypothesis—which also posited influences from India—was widely accepted. But contradictory evidence was not long in coming. In the 1930s, Dutch scholar F. D. K. Bosch took another look at the inscriptions on Indonesian monuments and observed that they made no mention of Indian incursions or conquests. Further, the linguistic and other signs of Indian influence were stronger in the inland kingdoms than in the coastal areas to which the Indians would have had easiest, first, and longest access. Both of these observations were at odds with the usual manifestations of progressive colonization and acculturation, but while they suggested that something was wrong with the traditional interpretation, they did not suggest a correct one.

At about the same time, the young Dutch historian Jacob Cornelis Van Leur was offering a possible explanation. Perhaps Indian culture had not overwhelmed and replaced the practices and beliefs of the local population; perhaps, instead, the established rulers and priests of the region had adopted those aspects of Indian language, ritual, and political organization that appealed to them. In that case, the proper way to look at such magnificent achievements as Angkor Wat, for example, would be to see Indian influence as an overlay, in Van Leur's metaphor a "thin and flaking glaze," on a previously existing, vibrant, indigenous culture.

Other contradictions to the traditional interpretation of the region's prehistory arose outside the specialties of archaeology and anthropology. Botanists studying the origins of domesticated plants had long speculated that a number of the world's major crops—including rice, yams, taro, sugarcane, and bananas—may have originated in Southeast Asia, perhaps earlier than previously suspected.

Indeed, in 1952, the American geographer Carl Sauer, citing the region's mild climate and wide variety of vegetation, suggested that it might have seen the birth of human agriculture. But there was as yet no archaeological evidence—no dated remains of early agriculture in the region—and the suggestions were dismissed by most experts.

For the two decades following World War II, virtually no archaeologist was looking for hard evidence of the indigenous, prehistoric Southeast Asian culture that would have preceded the historic civilizations. For one thing, it was assumed that the material culture of such people would have been largely organic and would thus have decomposed in the wet, tropical climate. For another, it was further assumed that if there had been any such people their existence would have been of little import to the region's development or to archaeology in general. It was possible to maintain this latter assumption despite the discovery of a few bronze and iron artifacts in early sites because they had been unearthed without the necessary rigorous attention to the stratification of the site—and without recourse to reliable dating. By the 1960s, however, archaeological procedures were improved, better technology was available, and all that was lacking was the interest. That was provided by the appearance on the Southeast Asian scene of a remarkable and controversial individual.

From his days as a graduate student of anthropology at the University of Arizona in the 1950s, Solheim had been intrigued by the missing prehistory of Southeast Asia. He helped organize the American branch of the loosely organized Far-Eastern Prehistory Association, now the International Indo-Pacific Prehistory Association, and became the first editor of its journal, *Asian Perspectives* (the first issue of which he published in 1957 on a mimeograph machine in the Tucson airport office where he was the night janitor).

As he pursued his later career as a professor at the University of Hawaii, Solheim may have looked the part of the typical archaeologist—in later years his bulk and beard would remind people of Santa Claus—but he did not act the part. He was fascinated by the arcane clues pointing to a substantial prehistory in Southeast Asia, embraced unconventional theories about it, and soon proclaimed, with what many of his more mainstream colleagues regarded as insufficient evidence and scholarship, the visionary idea that Southeast Asia was a major, early cradle of human civilization.

THE MOTHER OF ALL CHICKENS

The hotly colored red jungle fowl seen below runs wild in the tall grass of Thailand. But in 1994 a team of Japanese and American researchers discovered that a single subspecies of jungle fowl, *Gallus gallus gallus*, was domesticated in Southeast Asia more than 8,000 years ago, and that it is the maternal ancestor of all Western and Asiatic breeds of domestic chicken.

The researchers analyzed DNA samples from several breeds to reach this startling conclusion. Before, scientists thought Western domestic chickens descended from several Asian fowls that were domesticated in northeast China. The new finding corroborates other recent evidence that Southeast Asia may have been a nucleus of agricultural innovation.

Rice is thought to have been first cultivated along the Yangzi River in China, which was then considered part of Southeast Asia. And as early as 6,000 years ago, Southeast Asians were growing such staples as coconuts, yams, bananas, black pepper, and nutmeg; they were probably the first to domesticate these crops.

The boldness of Solheim's positions, along with the fervor of his search in the jungles and paddies of Southeast Asia for confirming evidence of prehistoric farmers, attracted students as unconventional as he. One of them was Chester Gorman, a Californian who gravitated to Solheim's classes at the University of Hawaii in 1961. Gorman's friends delighted in recalling that one of the things he did to earn money while working toward his degree in archaeology was some part-time gravedigging. In 1963, Gorman joined Solheim's team in making a last-minute survey for prehistoric sites in an area of northeast Thailand that was to be flooded by a series of dams being constructed on the tributary system of the Mekong River.

In 1965, Gorman returned to northern Thailand, near the Burmese border, to look for signs of Stone Age agriculture that might support Carl Sauer's theory. Gorman, on his way to becoming one of the few Western archaeologists to achieve fluency in the complex Thai language, covered the area on foot with one assistant. He stayed for several days in each village, asking people whether they knew of any caves or ancient artifacts. Near Mai Sang Nam in April 1966 local hunters showed him a three-chambered limestone cave overlooking the valley of the Kong. It was called Spirit Cave.

The shelter had clearly been used by ancient humans. Gorman found himself in a complex of three small, interconnected caves on different levels. The middle cave—which was about 35 feet by 25 feet with a ceiling sloping from 12 feet at the front to about 3 feet at the rear—held the treasure-trove. "The surface of the Spirit Cave deposit was very promising," Gorman wrote in a 1970 report whose scientific tone could not conceal his excitement; "large quartzite cores, flakes, and cord-marked sherds were immediately observable."

Excavating this rich site would be anything but easy. Getting to Spirit Cave took a three-day walk from the nearest transportation (a day's hike from the nearest sizable village), then a 600-foot climb up a steep limestone cliff. That climb had to be made every day, since camping in the cave was out of the question, and each day's supplies would have to be carried on the climbers' backs. The party's food supply consisted of all the rice they could carry in from the nearest village, plus whatever meat a hired hunter could bag in the nearby jungle. "There were many occasions," an associate recalled, "when the evening meal was boiled rice plus one or two frogs or snails."

Notwithstanding these privations, Gorman applied, for the first time at a Hoabinhian site, strict techniques and modern methodologies for stratigraphic control and meticulous excavation, screening, and recovery of every bit of human, animal, and plant remains to be found in the cave. The fieldwork was supported back in Hawaii by laboratory work that included radiocarbon dating, paleobotanical studies, and stone-tool analysis.

Five distinct layers of soil and detritus indicated that Spirit Cave had been used by humans for a period of about 5,000 years, beginning about 10,000 BC. The earliest human visitors had laid fires on the cave floor, with the logs radiating outward, and were apparently nomadic hunters using the cave for occasional shelter.

The sieving process yielded intriguing evidence. Chopped animal bones found around hearths showed no signs of charring, indicating that they were not roasted but perhaps prepared as a stew. Even more suggestive was the wide variety of plant remains—such things as beans, Chinese water chestnuts, bottle gourd, and a plant related to the cucumber—that, judging from radiocarbon analysis of surrounding materials, probably dated from the earliest through the final periods of habitation. Some attributes of the plant remains, including the large size of some of the seeds, indicated the possibility of an incipient stage of cultivation.

If so, then whoever cultivated the plants were among the world's first farmers. Gorman, however, was careful not to overstate this claim, saying only that the evidence indicated "a stage of plant exploitation beyond simple gathering."

Moreover, Gorman thought there was a different interpretation of the stone cobbles, which had at first been taken to be a more primitive form of stone tools than those in use in Europe at the same time. He suggested that it was simply a matter of resources: In the absence of fine-grained, easily flaked flint, the Hoabinhians had been forced to adopt a relatively simple technology based on the poorer quality, quartzite stone cobbles.

At the cave's 8,000-year level, Gorman found evidence that the people had begun making and using pottery of a well-developed kind, which was burnished, decorated with incised designs, and bore the marks of woven cords pressed into its surface. The significance of this change extends beyond the pottery itself; archaeologists are accustomed to seeing pottery develop in conjunction with agriculture.

Early in the 1970s, Chester Gorman pauses briefly during his northwestern Thailand search for more Hoabinhian cave sites, a gun for hunting and protection cradled in his arm. Gorman's survey took him through the dangerous opium and heroin trafficking area (encompassing parts of Thailand, Laos, and Burma) known as the Golden Triangle.

Along with the remains of this pottery, Gorman and his team found a number of stone tools, among them such things as small slate knives and rectangular utensils, that were of better quality than the usual river cobbles. One stone adze that dated to about 7000 BC had a polished surface created several millennia before any similarly advanced tool found in North China had been made. And yet, it had long been presumed that the Chinese had introduced polished and ground stone tools to Southeast Asia in about 3000 BC.

After taking three years to analyze and write about the Spirit Cave excavation, Gorman returned to Thailand in 1972 to look at other sites and get a picture of the settlement patterns. Excavations at Banyan Valley Cave and Steep Cliff Cave nearby confirmed that Spirit Cave had been no aberration—the Hoabinhian economy had flourished over a wide area from 10,000 BC to AD 1000. As remarkable as the Spirit Cave findings were, they did little more than hint that there might be something to the idea held by Solheim and others that prehistoric Southeast Asians had practiced early agriculture.

Harder evidence was soon forthcoming. During his survey of the Mekong dam project area, Gorman had discovered another prehistoric cemetery, later known as Non Nok Tha. In 1966, another Solheim student named Donn Bayard began an excavation at this unimposing mound of about three acres that rose a mere five feet above the surrounding rice paddies. Although Bayard went down only about four feet, he found 17 distinct levels of use.

With the very first results of the dating of Non Nok Tha, Solheim wrote later, "we began to realize what a truly revolutionary site this was. In a scrap of broken pottery little more than an inch square, we found an imprint of the husk of a grain of rice." Radiocarbon dating of the level above the sherd indicated that it could have dated from around 3500 BC,

Partly excavated squares stretch across the mouth of Thailand's Banyan Valley Cave during Chester Gorman's 1972-1973 dig, which turned up numerous Hoabinhian artifacts, small animal bones, and plant remains. Many of the smaller pieces were recovered when excavated dirt was sifted through circular screens like the one seen at lower right.

which at the time was "as much as a thousand years earlier than rice has been dated for either India or China—where, some archaeologists have claimed, rice was first domesticated."

By carefully exhuming, dating, and analyzing the contents of the descending sequence of graves at Non Nok Tha—which included human remains and grave goods, among them pieces of more than 800 pots—Bayard constructed a timeline of three general periods of occupation at Non Nok Tha. During the earliest, from 3500 BC to about 2000 BC—at a time when the first cities and empires were appearing in the fertile region between Mesopotamia's Tigris and Euphrates Rivers—he discovered no evidence of metal, with the exception of a single, mysterious, copper-alloy tool. Found lying on the rib cage of a middle-aged man who had been buried toward the end of the period, the tool was socketed, for mounting on a stick, but its function was unclear; it might have been a point for a digging stick. Whatever its use, its presence indicated that Southeast Asians had metal tools far earlier than anyone had guessed.

In the second period, which lasted well into the first millennium BC, bronze implements were found. Bayard unearthed bronze bracelets and axes, small lumps of bronze apparently spilled in casting, and sandstone molds for casting socketed axes. But, throughout this period no iron implements were found—confounding the theory that bronze and iron technology had been given to the Southeast Asians at the same time, about 500 BC. But the presence of iron implements in grave sites of the latest period of occupation, during the first millennium AD, shows that the durable metal was widely used by then.

There was nothing primitive or accidental about even the earliest metal objects of Non Nok Tha. Extensive analysis of the artifacts revealed that in most of the bronze pieces, the proportion of tin was in the narrow range—10 to 15 percent—that provides the best utilitarian properties of the alloy. Molecular structures of some of the tools, such as a nearly 4,000-year-old ax, show that the piece was formed by pouring the molten alloy into a mold; the edge was formed by hammering it out after the metal was cold; and finally the metal was annealed—

A VILLAGE TALE TOLD IN THE LAB

New Zealand and Thai archaeologists Charles Higham and Rachanie Thosarat spent seven months in 1985 excavating the prehistoric Thai village of Khok Phanom Di, near the Gulf of Thailand. But despite numerous burials, pottery pieces, rice fragments, shellfish remains, and other relics, the team as yet knew little about the village. Learning more would require further digging—in the lab.

In the following years, analysts found that about halfway through the village's 500-year existence (2000 to 1500 BC), life altered drastically. Skeletons

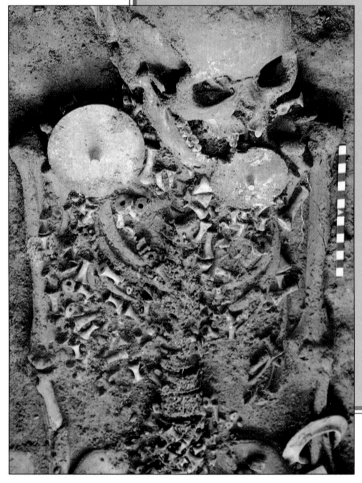

of male villagers offered striking evidence of this. Bone formations and joint-degeneration patterns indicated that early generations were robust and active. But later, men became weaker and more sedentary. Material artifacts also changed. Bone fishhooks and clay net weights, for instance, initially cropped up in numbers, but later disappeared from the site.

Interestingly, it was a 1991 shellfish study that gave Higham the key. A shift in the kinds of shellfish eaten, from mostly coastal and estuary species to freshwater types, suggested environmental change. Higham could now begin to reconstruct Khok Phanom Di's history. According to his theory, the village had been established on an estuary leading to the gulf. Villagers cultivated rice, and in the early years, the men reaped the protein-rich bounty of the nearby river and sea with hooks and nets. Gradually, silt built up, making access to the sea difficult. Then the river flooded and formed a new, distant channel. Fishing was now done inland, probably with bamboo cages. To survive, villagers turned to pottery trading, and potters, undoubtedly women, gained esteem. Such a master potter may have been the woman excavators named the Princess. A strong left wrist revealed her profession, as did the pottery implements and beautiful pots buried with her. Her status was also proclaimed by the 120,000 shell beads she wore *(left)*.

heated to a temperature high enough to reduce the brittleness caused by cold hammering, and then quickly cooled.

The confirmation of early metal technology in Southeast Asia posed a serious challenge to established scientific wisdom. Bayard called the accepted paradigm the "knowledgeable traveler" hypothesis, which attributed Southeast Asian development to benefactors from elsewhere. Non Nok Tha provided compelling, contrary evidence of what Bayard dubbed "inventive aborigines," who apparently learned about metallurgy largely on their own—or at the very least developed an indigenous, regionally distinctive technology.

Not surprisingly, the claims being made for Non Nok Tha did not go without challenge. It was, after all, the first field evidence of a hypothesis that threatened to overturn long and strongly held beliefs. Some of the dates yielded by technical analysis were contradictory, as often happens, and sorting out the precise chronology of four millennia compressed into a depth of only four feet was hardly straightforward. Other objections were raised because there was no evidence of any copper ore within 60 miles of the site, no explanation of how or where the artisans could have obtained it or of how or where they smelted it. If the notion of the inventive aborigine was to be taken seriously, it would have to be corroborated *(page 28)*.

I t was in this context that Stephen Young stumbled onto the pottery of Ban Chiang. The villagers were of course familiar with the bits of pottery that had always littered the ground of their village, but they had not thought much about the sherds before one of their number, in 1957, came upon an unbroken pot. Its great beauty and antiquity stimulated appreciation, comment, and a desire for more.

When news of the initial thermoluminescence testing of the pottery became public in 1970, the impression became widespread that all the pots were 6,000 years old, and both the discussion of the pottery in academic circles and its exhumation by villagers became overheated. By the time preparations had been made for a major scientific investigation of the buried treasure of Ban Chiang, it was difficult to find an undisturbed place to begin, since the villagers had been avidly digging up the pots and selling them. In fact, this organized looting had become a major village industry.

Froelich Rainey of the University of Pennsylvania Museum, who visited Ban Chiang in 1973, recalled watching "scores of the vil-

Thought to have been made nearly 4,000 years ago, this socketed bronze spearpoint, deliberately bent before being placed in a young man's grave at Ban Chiang, reveals a marked level of technological skill. The metalworker cast it with a two-piece mold, inserting a central piece to shape the socket, then hammered and annealed (heated) the edge to strengthen it.

lagers digging under their pile-supported houses in a kind of do-it-yourself archaeology. At house after house we climbed up a ladder to the veranda, took off our shoes, and while waiting for tea, examined our hosts' recent, unsold collections of pottery, bronze, iron, stone, and bone objects. Many of the less-decorated pots were left under the house to hold water and grain for the chickens—pots now worth several thousand dollars apiece." It took time and effort to find two undisturbed areas in the village, one along a village road and the other in the yard of a private citizen.

Finally, in 1974, actual excavation began *(pages 33-41)*. In contrast to the smaller projects at Spirit Cave and Non Nok Tha, this was a large undertaking by a partnership of American and Thai scholars. Funded by the University of Pennsylvania Museum and Thailand's Fine Arts Department, and directed by Chester Gorman and the Thai archaeologist Pisit Charoenwongsa, the team included not only senior officials and scholars from both parent organizations but also a number of specialists in such scientific disciplines as metallurgy, botany, paleozoology, and physical anthropology.

Moreover, the team had even broader objectives than the particular research at hand; they would be training an entire generation of Southeast Asian archaeologists in the latest methods of the science. All this posed daunting problems of administration. "A large and ever-growing organization," recalled a rueful Charoenwongsa, "inevitably resulted in the disorganization of its organizers."

Although the first item uncovered in the top stratum of the dig turned out to be a 20th-century toilet bowl, it was soon apparent to the excavators that Ban Chiang was a far richer site than anyone had expected. "The red-painted pottery that captured public opinion," American archaeologist Joyce White noted later, "was literally the tip of the iceberg." There were "many additional levels of deposit and a great variety of other equally distinctive ceramics." For thousands of years people had alternately lived and buried their dead on the site. The builders of each new settlement sank the pilings for their dwellings right through the graves of their predecessors.

More exciting than the wealth of pottery was the evidence of early metallurgy. Bronze artifacts were found beneath the levels of the famous red-painted pottery, but in decreasing numbers as the excavation proceeded. By the end of the first digging season, in 1974, the disappointed researchers were not finding any bronze at all. The next year, at another site, they came upon a completely different style of burial, in which the bodies were covered by layers of broken pottery. And some of these graves, wrote Joyce White, "unexpectedly produced unusual bimetallic objects, including two spearpoints with iron blades and bronze hafts, plus a bronze bangle encircled by iron rings. One five-year-old child wore several iron bracelets."

Again, as the diggers went lower, metal objects became rarer. No one knew exactly where they were in time, of course; that would not come until extensive analysis and dating had been done. Finally, at the end of the season, with the deep excavation pits threatening to cave in (and take nearby houses with them), Gorman spotted what looked like a bronze pin in the bottom of the excavation. Getting it out would be, he wrote in his notes, "a bit dicey," since the walls of the cramped space were about to give way and there was "no room to run." But the prize was worth the risk; when he gingerly removed it, he found it was no simple pin, but a socketed spearhead whose point had been deliberately bent, apparently as part of the funeral rite. Later analysis would show that it had been cast, cold hammered, and annealed—the same process used on the Non Nok Tha ax. "Our last and most dangerous" excavation, Gorman exulted, yielded "exactly what we hoped for in the bottom layer."

Also during the second season of digging at Ban Chiang they uncovered evidence of casting. At the level corresponding to about the mid-first millennium

The simple, yet exquisite, lines of this white ceramic pot dated between 800 and 400 BC demonstrate that the skill of pottery making in Ban Chiang did not begin with the famous red-on-buff pottery produced between 200 BC and AD 300. In modern times, this pot and others like it had to be carefully reassembled from many pieces because they had been deliberately shattered over a grave in a distinctive funeral ritual.

BC, excavators found the remains of clay crucibles and a large deposit of baked clay. The crucibles, their clay tempered with rice husks, contained traces of dross—impurities that separate from molten metal. Researchers speculated that the crucibles were filled with copper and tin ingots and fuel, and then placed in clay-lined pits, where the fuel was ignited and raised close to copper's melting point of 1,980°F. by means of a bellows—probably the traditional Southeast Asian piston type. The molten bronze was then poured into sandstone or lost-wax molds, evidence of which has been found at several sites.

In all, the excavations uncovered more than 120 graves. After two seasons of digging, the excavators shipped to the University of Pennsylvania Museum in Philadelphia containers, weighing 18 tons, filled with excavated materials—bits of pottery, metal, stone, soils, and charcoal—for analysis and dating. The human bones were sent to the University of Hawaii and the animal remains to the University of Otago in New Zealand. Before its eventual return to Thailand, the material was to be measured, weighed, sketched, classified, analyzed, and dated—and then everything, including each piece's point of origin in the excavations was recorded in a computer database.

For the first time, scientists could begin to establish a rigor-

SOLVING THE MYSTERY OF BRONZE PRODUCTION

After bronze implements in graves at prehistoric sites in Thailand came to light during the late 1960s and 1970s, archaeologists began to examine the possibility that copper- and bronze-making technology might have developed in Southeast Asia and not been imported from elsewhere in Asia, as had been thought. But then where were the ancient sources of copper and tin, the ingredients of bronze, and where had the smelting gone on?

To find out, the Thailand Archaeometallurgy Project (TAP) got under way. In 1984, American and Thai archaeologists Vincent Pigott and Surapol Natapintu surveyed northeast Thailand for ores. They identified a copper-mining site, the second- and first-millennium-BC site of Phu Lon (right). Exploration in 1985 revealed that the miners had dug and smelted carbonate ore of copper—a greenish mineral called malachite. They had crushed the rock with hand-held stones to extract the malachite in the quartz matrix. The excavators found an abundance of charcoal, in amounts needed to smelt copper. Two mold fragments and more than 70 small ceramic crucible fragments showed that some casting had also been carried out here.

More recent research on the Bangkok Plain has enabled TAP archaeologists to document all the major steps in the process of prehistoric metal production, demonstrating that ancient Southeast Asia indeed developed a distinctive bronze-making technology.

ous timeline for settled village life reaching more than 5,000 years into the prehistory of Southeast Asia. And ironically enough, the analysis showed that the first dating of the distinctive red-painted pottery—which had ignited the fervor of collectors and archaeologists alike—had been wrong. The thermoluminescence technique had been experimental at the time, and it was applied to pots of uncertain provenance. Far from being 6,000 years old, the pottery was associated with the most recent period of the prehistoric culture of Ban Chiang, from about 300 BC to AD 200. But this hardly quenched interest in the site, for the analysis showed that the people who in their later period produced the painted pottery had thrived on that site for the previous 2,000 to 3,000 years, and during that entire period they had produced pottery that was unusually beautiful.

Ban Chiang and contemporary villages later discovered on the

Excavation equipment and thatched shelters surround a 75-foot-high pinnacle at Thailand's Phu Lon, the skeletal remains of the ancient mining works. The ladders were used by excavators to enter a few deep pockets, or soundings, from which the ore was dug. Still visible on the surface is the green of residual oxidized-copper ore deposits.

As rust developed around them, kernels of rice were to leave their mark on the piece of prehistoric iron above, found during the Ban Chiang excavations of 1974 and 1975. Similar impressions on pottery excavated there suggest that an intermediate form of rice, neither fully wild nor totally domesticated, was raised by the ancient inhabitants of the site.

Khorat Plateau of northeastern Thailand were seemingly tranquil farming and hunting communities established by people who moved into the region during the fourth millennium BC. Where they orginated remains a mystery, but it is thought that they came from farther upstream in the Mekong watershed. With its subtropical climate and six-month rainy season, the plateau offered a wide variety of plant and animal life, of which the Ban Chiang settlers made full use. But before these pioneers ever arrived on the plateau, they had progressed beyond simple hunting and gathering. The earliest settlers did many things not permitted by the nomadic life of hunter-gatherers: They lived in villages of thatched houses built on pilings; they made heavy and fragile pottery; and they had domestic cattle, pigs, and chickens *(pages 20-21)*. In addition, they had dogs—clear evidence of their immigration, since wolves, to which dogs are related, did not occur indigenously in Thailand. The villagers probably cultivated rice from the very beginning of their residence (their earliest pottery contains embedded rice husks), although they did it, at least initially, without use of water buffalo to draw their plows.

As remarkable as this early agriculture was, the dates assigned to Ban Chiang's metallurgy were even more startling. The research indicated that the village may have had a well-developed local bronze technology by about 2000 BC, roughly the same time that bronze-working became common in China. The oldest artifacts found at the site show considerable competence in bronzeworking, and the later appearance of high-tin bronze and more ornately crafted pieces indicates a high degree of vitality and innovation in metallurgy.

Moreover, in addition to a bronze age, Ban Chiang had clearly experienced an iron age. Dating to the first half of the first millennium BC, the iron bangles and spearpoints found at Ban Chiang may be "some of the oldest iron objects in East Asia," according to Joyce White. And they imply an impressive forging technology different from that used to produce bronze. The melting temperature of iron is more than 800°F. higher than that of copper. But iron ore can be smelted—that is, heated close enough to melting so that impurities can be separated by forging, or beating, at a temperature roughly comparable to that required to melt copper. The metal from the earliest iron artifacts found in China had been extracted from meteorites, and had already been "smelted" by the heat of the meteorite's fiery passage through the atmosphere. But analysis of the Ban Chiang iron indicates that it was deliberately smelted from ores.

In 1981, Ban Chiang resident Li Hiri-onatha, a self-taught naturalist, readies another botanical specimen for pressing between sheets of newspaper while American archaeologist Joyce White takes notes on each plant's properties. The stack of pressed samples will be bound in the bamboo frame at right, dried, and sent back to the University of Pennsylvania Museum for further analysis. Such ethnobotanical studies of the modern vegetation in the vicinity of ancient sites can help researchers to reconstruct prehistoric village farming, plant usages, and environments.

Certain cultural aspects of the Ban Chiang metallurgy were as startling as the presence of the technology. Unlike Mesopotamia and China, where advances in metallurgy seemed to have been driven by military needs and expressed in the form of weapons or icons of battle, at Ban Chiang the uses of metals were almost exclusively utilitarian and ornamental. As millennia passed, change was gradual and undramatic in the village of Ban Chiang, seen mostly in new burial practices, the evolution of metals technology, and an increasing level of affluence. Moreover, metals were apparently not reserved for the wealthy—fine metal ornaments were found often on the arms and legs of children. Thus researchers were faced with the further anomaly that the advances in Southeast Asia had not been driven by strife or political centralization, but they had been arrived at relatively peacefully, and in an evolutionary rather than revolutionary manner.

Indeed, Ban Chiang shows no evidence of any of those factors commonly regarded as necessary spurs to innovation and human

progress. There is no sign of climatic stress, of disaster, or of special advantages such as nearby deposits of natural resources, either precious or utilitarian. Yet no other site excavated so far in Thailand offers the quantity or quality of material remains across such a time depth as found in Ban Chiang. It seemed to be, wrote Joyce White, "a regional center—but a center for what?"

Many questions remain about the remarkable prehistoric people of Ban Chiang, including how they came to know about metals—and where they obtained them—and how much influence they had on technological advancement elsewhere in the region. But their significance in the history of their region has been established. And in the words of Joyce White, addressing the implications of the broader research into Southeast Asian prehistory, "it can no longer be denied that social and economic developments in the region from prehistory onward" have had a profound and far-flung impact.

While specific evidence of the manner in which metalworking technology spread has yet to be discovered, there is one area—the settlement of countless southern Pacific islands—where the impact of events starting in Southeast Asia seems clear. Linguistic studies have documented the outward spread from the region of Austronesian languages, 6,000 years old or more, containing words implying rice cultivation and the use of metal tools. The eventual range of this language, extending more than halfway around the world, from Madagascar to Easter Island, offers the earliest known evidence of a culture advanced enough to have dispersed across the seas.

The view of Southeast Asia as a cradle, rather than a repository, of human advancement has not yet been fully established three decades after the discovery of Ban Chiang. The monumental task of analyzing, checking, and cross-referencing the volumes of material excavated there, and at other sites found in the succeeding years, continues. Sadly, in the midst of the excitement created by his discoveries at Spirit Cave and Ban Chiang, Chet Gorman died in 1981, at the age of 43. His place at the head of the American team working on Ban Chiang was taken by Joyce White, who had been pursuing her graduate studies while engaged in the project. It has been left to Gorman's successors, a growing international body of archaeologists from the United States, New Zealand, Thailand, Australia, Europe, and elsewhere, a group of what Gorman cheerfully labeled "Southeast Asian chauvinists," to confirm whether they are at work in a backwater, or a cradle, of human civilization.

READING AN ANCIENT STORY

During the early 1970s, archaeologists raced against illicit diggers to recover the prehistoric artifacts lying beneath the village of Ban Chiang, Thailand. But while their rivals saw only prizes to be snatched, the archaeologists imagined, in the words of one, "a giant history book, waiting to be read." In 1974 a joint expedition from the Thai Fine Arts Department and the University of Pennsylvania Museum journeyed to the northeastern village in hopes of deciphering the story.

Although the Fine Arts Department had sponsored earlier excavations, this joint endeavor was a "multidiscipline, multinational attack," according to its Thai and American codirectors, Pisit Charoenwongsa and Chester Gorman. Specialists from countries around the world brought their expertise to Ban Chiang, arriving at different periods for fieldwork and departing at various times for laboratory analysis back home.

In its role as a model, the Ban Chiang dig was a training ground for students and young professionals eager to learn the latest archaeological techniques. Villagers hired to assist received their own instruction, and some of them became valuable team members. (Several can be seen above excavating under the thatch-roofed structure built to protect the site.) The photographic record of excavations at Ban Chiang—the basis of this picture essay—not only tracks one of the most momentous digs in the study of prehistoric Southeast Asia but also shows what archaeologists do in the field.

Having descended into excavation square D7 on June 10, 1975, Filipino archaeologist-trainee Lionel Chiong uncovers an infant's skull and ribs using a dental pick (right hand) and a blower. The diagram identifies various items in the photo, including a skeleton chart upon which bones found were marked in red (A); a bag for finds, individually numbered and dated, with the square, level, and burial where they lay noted (B); vertebrae and other skeletal fragments (C); dental picks (D); pointing trowels (E); dustpan (F); brush (G); charcoal specimen in foil for radiocarbon dating (H); regular trowel (I); and ribs (J).

EXACTING WORK DEEP IN THE GROUND

Ban Chiang's excavators dug when the weather was "hot, hotter, and hottest," as one phrased it. During the monsoon season, rains battered the thatched roof overhead and necessitated the building of small earthen dams around the site to keep it from being inundated.

Working six days a week, archaeologists and students, assisted by villagers, excavated, recorded, cleaned, and sorted during the day and analyzed and cataloged their finds at night.

The density of artifacts was "unbelievable" according to excavator William Schauffler. "Every time you moved your trowel, you found something." Freeing the finds often required the use of such tools as brushes and dental picks.

The discovery of a burial never failed to draw everyone on site to the spot. So Ban Chiang itself attracted the curious, among them tourists who peppered the excavators with questions as they watched the archaeologists retrieve bits and pieces of the distant past. As Schauffler recalled 20 years later of discovering this hitherto-unknown chapter in Southeast Asia's history, "It was an exciting time to be there."

To extract bone fragments, sherds, and other small items, a Ban Chiang villager (left) sifts dirt through a screen of one-centimeter wire mesh fitted in a wood frame, which hangs suspended from a bamboo rail. All soil excavated during the two seasons was sieved.

Pisit Charoenwongsa (below, on the left) observes as U.S. graduate students Louis Flamm (center) and William Schauffler pour excavated dirt into a froth-flotation machine. Light organic material floats to the surface, bouyed by rising air bubbles, leaving mud behind.

Photographed on May 16, 1975, square D4, separated into quadrants by string, shows a half-removed skeleton at lower right and an unusual oblong feature of standing pottery sherds, only partially excavated, at upper left. Two sticks measuring two meters (about 6½ feet) in length offer vertical and horizontal scale. To capture all details, archaeologists usually shoot dig photos in black-and-white as well as color, using different light settings.

A detailed field drawing, executed by American student Deborah Kramer, shows square D4's features on May 12, 1975. Although the key at far right tentatively identifies the standing sherds at upper left as a "pottery coffin," field notes made three days later admit it is "still a mystery." Further excavation eventually revealed not a coffin but the remains of an infant overlaid with ritually smashed pottery.

A Thai archaeologist measures the location of a feature within a quadrant before recording it on the graph paper attached to her clipboard. Such drawings were made approximately every four inches of depth, a unit of measurement chosen to define each level within a thicker soil stratum in the excavation. When the dig ended, the archaeologists had gone down about 13 feet.

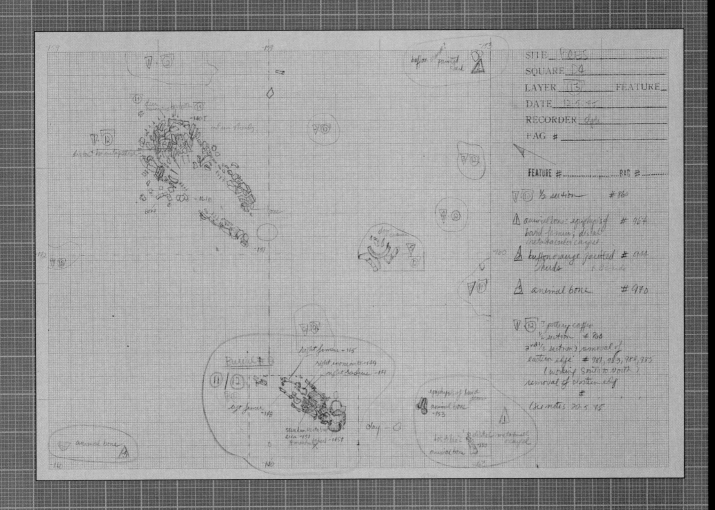

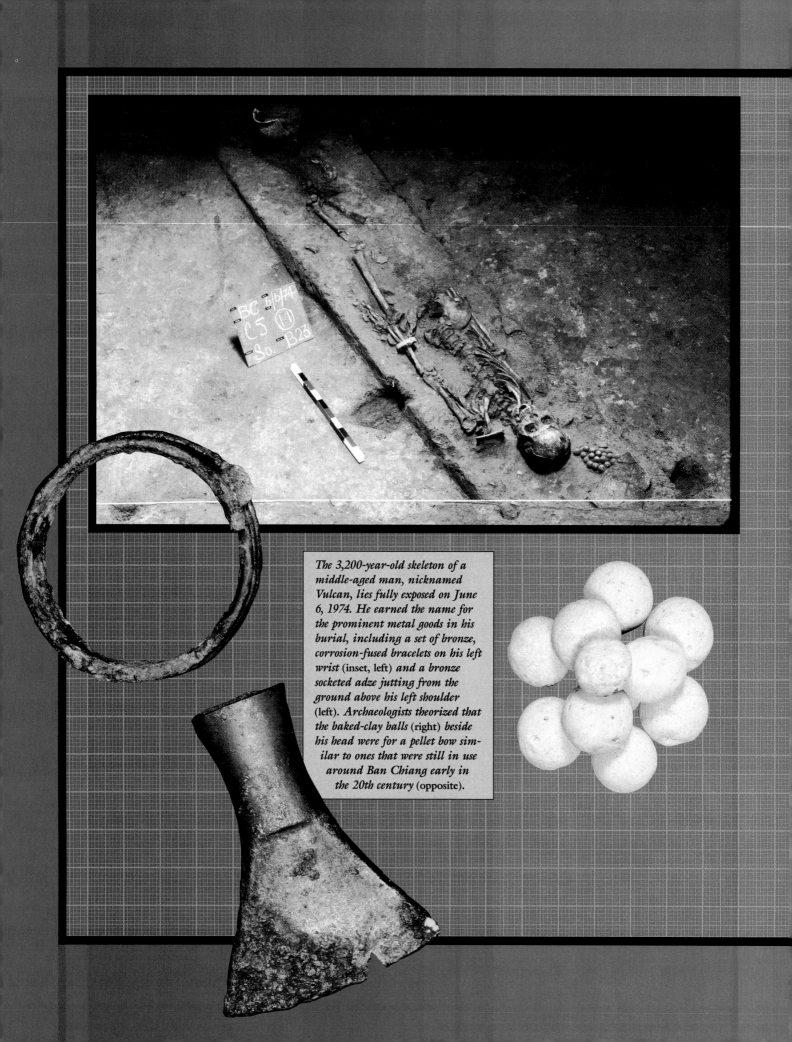

The 3,200-year-old skeleton of a middle-aged man, nicknamed Vulcan, lies fully exposed on June 6, 1974. He earned the name for the prominent metal goods in his burial, including a set of bronze, corrosion-fused bracelets on his left wrist (inset, left) *and a bronze socketed adze jutting from the ground above his left shoulder* (left). *Archaeologists theorized that the baked-clay balls* (right) *beside his head were for a pellet bow similar to ones that were still in use around Ban Chiang early in the 20th century* (opposite).

In Ban Om Kaeo, not far from Ban Chiang, a village elder weaves the small platform of rattan that will cradle the projectile of a now-rare pellet bow. The platform—which sits between a split string—and its ball were grasped and pulled back for firing by the archer, who used the weapon to hunt small animals and to herd water buffalo.

During the final days of the Ban Chiang dig, in September 1975, archaeologists excavate the balks, or walls, between already-explored areas, which were left standing to reveal the vertical sequence, or stratigraphy, of the site's natural and cultural deposits. Not all the balks were taken down; soon after this photograph was made, part of a side wall collapsed, making further digging precarious.

Thai excavators, using a diagram of a skeleton to aid in sorting bones for packing, prepare Ban Chiang's human remains for shipment to the University of Hawaii. Physical anthropologist Michael Pietrusewsky's ongoing analysis there has provided a detailed picture of the village's prehistoric residents, who in general were moderately tall and muscular, with large, rather broad heads and prominent faces.

Some 3,400 bags of sherds from Ban Chiang engulf Thai archaeologist Vidja Intakosai and William Schauffler in a village shed. The 1.25 million sherds were shipped from there to the University of Pennsylvania Museum to be analyzed and cataloged before their return to Thailand.

THE HAUNTING LEGACY OF BURIED DRUMS

The 60-foot-long, double voyaging canoe hoisted its square sail into the trade winds and gained way, nosing out onto the open ocean from its home port of Hilo, Hawaii. Without navigation instruments of any kind—not so much as a compass or sextant—the canoe was bound for Tahiti, a speck of an island 2,000 miles to the southeast. But in another sense the builders and sailors of the craft were embarked on a voyage back in time.

They were the Polynesian Voyaging Society, recruited and led by Ben Finney, chairman of the department of anthropology at the University of Hawaii. Their craft (christened *Hokule'a,* or "Arcturus," after their steering star for the voyage to Tahiti) was their approximation of the kind of vessel that might have been used by the blue-water sailors of Polynesia a few millennia before.

It was, admittedly, a rough guess. The twin hulls (made of plywood, not hollowed logs, as the originals would have been) were lashed (using synthetic lines, not coconut fiber) to crossbeams that supported a deck and two masts (for hoisting sails of fabric, not woven leaves). No pattern for such a canoe had ever been found in an archaeological dig—the constituent materials of the original models would have been organic and decayed quickly—and no recorded sketch or description existed that predated the era of European exploration. But Finney and his students had reasoned backward from

An eerie countenance from Indonesia, this Javanese death mask preserves the features of the face it once covered. Whether a sign of status, familial respect, or a way of containing a malevolent spirit, funerary masks represent the earliest use of gold in the Indonesian archipelago.

18th-century European observations, with full knowledge of the skills and technology of the people of the Pacific islands, and were fairly certain they had a reproduction of a Stone Age voyaging canoe.

Its mission, on this summer day in 1976, was what Finney would later call a voyage of rediscovery, an attempt to see how the islands of the South Pacific originally had been discovered and settled. It was also a voyage of denial: No less an authority than the noted Norwegian explorer Thor Heyerdahl had declared, after making a similar voyage in the famed *Kon-Tiki* in 1947, that ancient mariners could have found the little islands of Polynesia only by accident, as they ran before the region's prevailing easterly trade winds—so called because early European traders had utilized them to sail around the tip of Africa from the east on their way back to home port. Thus, he concluded, they could have come only from Peru.

The problem remained that the languages and ethnicity of the islanders did not resemble those of Peru, but those of Southeast Asia, thousands of miles downwind. To discover, colonize, and later trade with the islands, the settlers would have had to be capable of navigating thousands of miles of open water, against the trade winds. Was it possible? Ben Finney decided that the only way to find out was "to reconstruct the ancient voyaging canoes, relearn the old ways of navigating, and then test these on the long sea roads of Polynesia."

After an extensive search for someone with the traditional navigating skills of Polynesian islanders, Finney found Mau Piailug, from the Caroline Islands. Piailug could make his way at sea without compass, map, or sextant, orienting himself at night by the rising and setting points of certain stars and constellations, in the early morning and late afternoon by the position of the sun, and at midday or in overcast conditions by the direction of the dominant ocean swells. He kept a picture in his head of where he was in his journey by remembering the wind and current conditions he had encountered along the way and correcting his course periodically to compensate for drift. He watched for signs of landfall—distant clouds building up over land, for example, or disturbances in the pattern of the swells.

Most modern observers scoffed at the notion that such methods could guide a canoe between points a few hundred, let alone a few thousand, miles apart. Experts insisted that the inaccuracies inherent in every step, from estimating the bearing to a star or the sun without an instrument to calculating the effect of cross winds and currents, would accumulate rapidly and make accurate navigation im-

Relying solely on wind, wave, and stars for navigation in a craft built entirely from natural materials, the 12-person crew of Hawai'iloa *set sail from Hawaii in the spring of 1995. Named for the legendary discoverer of Hawaii, the 57-foot-long, twin-hulled canoe was constructed as part of an experiment to see whether prehistoric sailors of Southeast Asian stock could have settled islands of the South Pacific using such boats.*

possible. But Piailug and the Voyaging Society not only reached Tahiti and then returned to Hawaii in 1976 but repeated the voyage in 1980. They then went on to make several other voyages that by 1993 totaled 50,000 nautical miles on the open ocean, without instruments, charts, or other aids. Along the way, they had also recruited additional navigators, among them the Hawaiian Nainoa Thompson.

Explaining why the experts had been wrong about accumulating errors in navigation took some sophisticated analysis. While Finney's voyaging canoe carried no instruments that could be used on board, it did carry, sealed in one of its bows, a transponder with which the actual position of the canoe was tracked by satellite for later study. During a 1980 crossing to Tahiti, for example, the canoe was thrust 90 miles west of its course by a narrow current jet of which

Thompson was unaware. He thus assumed that the canoe was sailing 90 miles to the east of its actual course. Eleven days thereafter, overestimating the effects of the wide South Equatorial Current, he assumed that his position was 90 miles to the west, thus putting his dead-reckoning position almost on *Hokule'a*'s actual course. The experts had been right to believe that the errors of dead reckoning in long journeys were unavoidable. But they are not necessarily cumulative; they are random and to a great extent self-canceling.

Even after four voyages to Tahiti and back to Hawaii, however, Thor Heyerdahl's objection—that such primitive craft could not have sailed directly against the prevailing trade winds—still stood. While Tahiti is 2,000 miles south of Hawaii, it is only about 300 miles to eastward, or windward, into the trade winds. With its small sail area, shallow draft, and lack of a deep keel or centerboard, the voyaging canoe had limited ability to sail into the wind. It could manage a course of about 75 degrees off the wind, compared with the 50 degrees attained by modern racing yachts. Thus, Finney noted, in order to sail just 500 miles directly against the prevailing wind and current a canoe would have to be tacked back and forth for a total distance of considerably more than 2,000 miles. And a voyage from the islands of Indonesia to Tahiti would involve traversing one-third of

Builders of Hawai'iloa *hollow out a giant log that will serve as one of the vessel's two hulls. One hundred volunteers worked for days to chisel more than 6,000 pounds of shavings from the two Sitka spruce trunks used. The 400-year-old trees were a gift from Alaska. Prehistoric Pacific mariners had access to such wood, in the form of logs that washed into the sea along the Alaska coast and were carried on ocean currents to Pacific beaches. Hawaiians viewed such logs as having been bestowed by the gods.*

the circumference of the planet, directly against the prevailing trade winds and ocean currents.

"The solution to this apparent dilemma," wrote Finney, required neither high technology nor abstract reasoning. The simple fact was that "the trades do not always blow. They periodically die down and are replaced by spells of westerly winds." The presumptive Stone Age voyagers could have just waited for these contrary winds in order to ride them eastward. In fact, that method had been described to the 18th-century English explorer Captain James Cook by his Tahitian guide, and although Cook made a record of the conversation, it was little noticed until Finney and his voyagers confirmed it during a two-year, 12,000-mile voyage through the islands beginning in 1985. Sometimes running before the wind at 12 knots, other times becalmed or beached by contrary winds, *Hokule'a* made an average of 100 miles per day on its long voyages. Moreover, Finney wrote afterward with obvious pride, "We have been able to sail her exactly where we wanted to go."

Indeed, in early 1995, *Hokule'a* set forth on another voyage, this time with a sister ship christened *Hawai'iloa*. Unlike the much-traveled *Hokule'a*, this new 57-foot voyager was made mostly of wood, and its sails were woven out of the sword-shaped leaves of the pandanus tree. The two vessels sailed to the island of Huahine, 150 miles west of Tahiti; there they were joined by traditional seagoing canoes from Tahiti, New Zealand, and the Cook Islands. The little flotilla went on to Tahiti, the Marquesas Islands, and then back to Hawaii, adding more proof to the notion that early Southeast Asian mariners could have set sail for distant Pacific islands.

The spread of Southeast Asian language and culture—and the sophisticated geographic and navigational knowledge implied in the ancient migration to far-flung locales—is additional evidence pointing to Southeast Asia's having been far more, in prehistoric times, than a mere passive receptor of the cultural and technological advances of other peoples. Added to the archaeological evidence from such sites as Spirit Cave and Ban Chiang, Finney's voyages helped emphasize the importance of reevaluating longstanding assumptions about the prehistory of Southeast Asia. But such revisions would have to deal with the objections of traditionally oriented scientists— that advocates of change were relying too much on speculation about what might have happened, that there was no broad-based, conventional archaeological record supporting the new ideas. Only a very

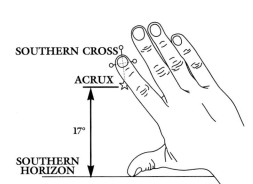

A diagram shows how navigation by the stars is possible. By placing his thumb on the southern horizon and his index finger between the four stars that form the Southern Cross, Hawaiian navigator Nainoa Thompson learned to calculate the latitude of a seagoing craft's position. He knew, for instance, that Acrux is 27° above the horizon at the equator; thus, if he observed Acrux at 17°, as here, he realized he must be at 10° north latitude. Through years spent studying Hawaiian sea and sky patterns, Thompson reinvented the lost skill that would be used successfully aboard Hawai'iloa *and her sister vessel,* Hokule'a.

SOUTHERN CROSS

ACRUX

17°

SOUTHERN HORIZON

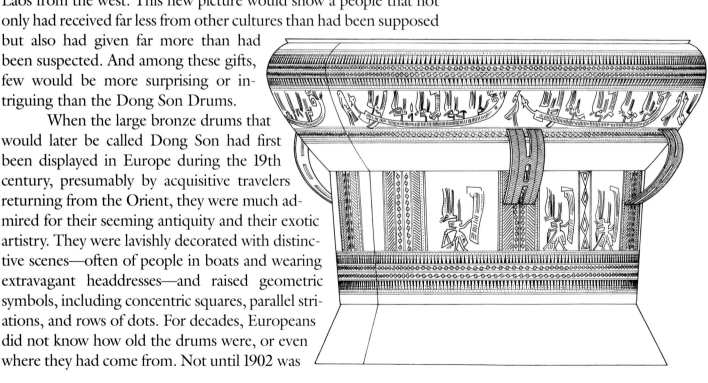

few sites, such as Ban Chiang, were presenting a long, continuous, and verifiable record of local, prehistoric cultural development. Finding and interpreting others, in the midst of the armed conflicts that flared continually throughout the region, would be difficult at best.

Nevertheless, evidence of the region's prehistoric vigor would accumulate throughout the 1970s and 1980s, especially as a new generation of native-born archaeologists, energized by the dawning realization of their own powerful heritage, embraced and authenticated the new ideas with increasing fervor. Aided by such nontraditional data as that accumulated by the seafaring adventures of Ben Finney and the studies of linguists, they are sketching an increasingly detailed picture of the people who lived in Southeast Asia before the Chinese arrived from the northeast to dominate part of what is today northern Vietnam, and before Indian trade goods and religions spread into Burma, Thailand, Cambodia, and Laos from the west. This new picture would show a people that not only had received far less from other cultures than had been supposed but also had given far more than had been suspected. And among these gifts, few would be more surprising or intriguing than the Dong Son Drums.

When the large bronze drums that would later be called Dong Son had first been displayed in Europe during the 19th century, presumably by acquisitive travelers returning from the Orient, they were much admired for their seeming antiquity and their exotic artistry. They were lavishly decorated with distinctive scenes—often of people in boats and wearing extravagant headdresses—and raised geometric symbols, including concentric squares, parallel striations, and rows of dots. For decades, Europeans did not know how old the drums were, or even where they had come from. Not until 1902 was it established that they had been made in Southeast Asia, and it was 1929 before archaeologists reported finding examples of the distinctive drums in northern Vietnam—at a place called Dong Son, south of Hanoi—that some scholars dated to about the first century AD. Thereafter, similar drums were reportedly found throughout mainland and island Southeast Asia and south China.

The drums revealed a great deal about the Dong Son people, who occupied the delta of the Red River during the first millennium BC. The craftsmen had decorated the drums densely with scenes taken from their lives, depicting, for example, incidents of warfare—warriors wearing elaborate feather headdresses being borne into battle on elegant boats fitted with cabins and fighting platforms—and interludes of music, with the drums being played in sets of two or four, accompanied by other instruments. Aside from the fact that they represented a remarkably advanced metallurgy—casting such large, thin-walled, and densely decorated objects was a major technological feat—and artistry, one of the most intriguing facts about the drums was that such valuable artifacts had been interred with the dead. The graves of well-to-do Dong Son people often held pairs of full-size drums, while smaller versions, just as intricately worked, were used as burial urns for cremated remains or, sometimes, for severed heads.

The first drums to be dated may have been made during the first century AD, more than a century after the Chinese descended on the area, and it was long assumed that it was they who brought to the area a knowledge of metallurgy and other aspects of civilization. Chinese texts recalling the history of the early Han dynasty in the second century BC lent support for this traditional attitude by referring to the Dong Son people to their southwest as barbarians.

But when archaeologists applied modern research techniques to the contents of the Dong Son graves (which, because of the acidity of the soil, seldom contained any trace of human remains), they soon profiled a society, dating to the first millennium BC, that had enjoyed the benefits of such cultural and technological advances as irrigated rice cultivation with draft animals, metallurgy, fine craftsmanship, and a centralized and specialized society—all long before the advent of the Han Chinese. Indeed, the Dong Son people's culture appeared to have hit its stride a full four centuries before the Chinese appeared in their land.

Known by the ancient Chinese as Masters of the Drums, the Dong Son people were superb metallurgists who cast hundreds of decorated ceremonial drums, such as this 2½-foot-high example (left). *The 14-pointed star on the tympanum likely represents the sun; boats laden with plumed warriors on the drum's side* (drawing) *emphasize the Dong Son people's water-oriented society.*

Explaining how an indigenous Southeast Asian people achieved such an advanced metallurgy and culture had been a problem for skeptical scholars from the time the origin of the Dong Son drums was identified. During the 1930s, a debate had raged between two students of the region's prehistory. Austrian Robert Heine-Geldern and Bernard Karlgren, a Swede, disagreed by a few centuries on the date of the rise of the Dong Son culture and on the identity of the people who had brought the art form of the drums to Southeast Asia. But neither questioned that the distinctive geometric style of the art—along with the technology for working it in bronze—had been brought to the region by a "civilized" foreign benefactor. Each of them had located similar stylistic elements in the pottery or artifacts of other prehistoric cultures considered better qualified to be progenitors of a style as advanced as Dong Son. Heine-Geldern thought it had begun in Europe and had been brought to Asia sometime after 800 BC; Karlgren argued that it had come from central China and dated to the fourth or third centuries BC.

Archaeologists began to question the reasoning of Heine-Geldern and Karlgren when it became obvious that artistic motifs similar to Dong Son ones could be found among older Southeast Asian cultures. The discovery of an earlier indigenous bronze metallurgical tradition, first at Non Nok Tha in Thailand and later at many other sites in mainland Southeast Asia showed that the production of bronze artifacts preceded the Dong Son period by 1,000 years or

Marked by a spearhead, the tympanum of a bronze Dong Son drum (above) lies where archaeologist Olov Janse uncovered it in a tomb in the 1930s. Measuring almost 18 inches in diameter, it had been "killed," or ritually broken, before being sealed away. The plentiful bronze funeral deposits around the tympanum suggest that the grave was that of a Dong Son chieftain.

more. The study of Non Nok Tha and, by 1989, more than 30 similar sites, pointed to antecedent Southeast Asian cultures, such as one called Phung Nguyen, in northern Vietnam, which dated to about 2000 BC. This evidence placed the deeper roots of the Dong Son culture on its home ground, to the earliest settled villages in the region.

With the Red River Delta area torn by conflict for three decades after World War II, archaeological study of the Dong Son people was intermittent at best. Nevertheless, Vietnamese researchers made progress, and their findings became more widely known after peace returned to the country in 1975. Modern analysis and dating established that the Dong Son people and their predecessors had flourished in the region for at least 1,000 years before their subjugation by the Han Chinese.

Graves from the cultures preceding the classic Dong Son, dating roughly from 1000 to 500 BC, held mostly pottery. In the middle of the first millennium BC, bronze artifacts proliferated; not only drums but bucket-shaped situlae, lamps, dagger hilts, axes, plowshares, and ornaments. At one Dong Son site, Co Loa northwest of Hanoi, a walled, moated settlement of nearly 250 acres, a bronze drum was unearthed that weighed 160 pounds, which would have required the smelting of more than a ton of copper ore. Only during the late Dong Son, in the first century BC, did the burial goods begin to include Chinese artifacts such as coins, seals, and mirrors.

The Dong Son culture, with its distinctive drums, was for many decades the best-known example of Southeast Asian civiliza-

Prepared for the afterlife, this Dong Son male was laid to rest in a log coffin with a spear and axheads, a bamboo ladle, and a pottery vessel tucked between his legs. The find was made at Chau Can, one of many Dong Son-era sites that have been excavated since the 1960s and have yielded log coffins of the elite. While not as sumptuous as the burial at left, the warrior's grave preserved his skeleton, rare in the highly acidic soil of the region.

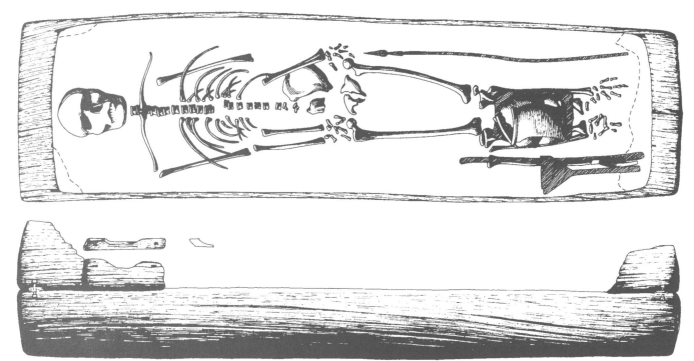

tion in the first millennium BC. And while it appeared to be substantially richer than its neighboring contemporaries—it enjoyed proximity not only to nearby deposits of copper and tin but also to overland trading routes—it was hardly alone. Other cultures were thriving in what is now Vietnam, one of them centered on the east-central coast and another in the south. Others were in northeast and central Thailand, and, it soon developed, yet another drum culture had evolved in what is now south China.

Located northwest of the Tonkin Plain in today's Yunnan Province of south China, the Dian culture may have been even richer than that of the Dong Son. This region prospered in the fertile Lake Dian basin from about 1000 BC and during the third and second centuries BC interacted with the Han Chinese, who viewed the southerners as barbarians. The Han subdued the Dian in 109 BC.

The Dian people preserved evidence of their ritual practices and religious beliefs in detailed, three-dimensional tableaux on the drums and drum-shaped containers for cowrie shells that have permitted modern archaeologists to infer more about the role and importance of the instrument in their society. For example, one small scene found on a burial drum depicted a wooden-pillared house around which 13 people are preparing food, playing music, and conducting a ritual that is no doubt related to the presence, inside the

Singers and musicians adorn this 3½-inch-high gilded-bronze buckle, found in one of 50 royal Dian tombs excavated between 1955 and 1960. Drummers and flutists accompany the top row of robed and earringed singers in crownlike hats. Like their Dong Son neighbors to the southeast, the Dian would ultimately see their drum culture subsumed by the Han.

otherwise empty house, of a severed human head on a post. Another, more complex scene is centered around a stack of drums beside which stands a female—obviously someone of status—who is being offered a drink by another, kneeling female. Around them are several other groupings: A large male, surrounded by standing and kneeling figures bearing containers of fish, grain, fruit, and vegetables, is tied to a post; a large woman surrounded by other figures is carried on a litter by a pair of males; other figures lead domestic animals.

From such representations, and from evidence of relict practices surviving in the region today, researchers have pieced together a picture of a people for whom the drum played a vital role in ensuring the fertility of their fields and their ability to communicate with spirits. Communication with the spirit world that permeated the natural features around them was essential to spiritual health and possible only through the sound of the drum. This connection between

One hundred twenty-seven figures crowd the 12-inch-wide bronze lid of a drum-shaped cowrie container unearthed in a Dian cemetery. (Such shells served as a form of currency among the Dian.) Under the roofed platform sit 16 drums, probably part of an allegiance ceremony that would have included human and animal sacrifice. Common in southwest China at the time, such blood-letting may have been intended as a ritual fertilization of the earth.

the people, the drums, nature, and the dead helps explain why such valuable instruments were buried in graves.

The evidence of the Dong Son drums shows that when the Han Chinese invaded the Tonkin Plain they found not barbarians but a mature society. Far from being a passive receptor of Chinese culture, the Dong Son way of life was well established and vigorous.

At about the time of the discovery of Ban Chiang, an archaeological team began a similarly important dig on the hills of Thailand's Chao Phraya plains. In 1957, archaeologist Chin You-di of Bangkok's National Museum had noted the existence, in a remote, overgrown location in extreme west-central Thailand, of a cave that in all probability contained valuable prehistoric artifacts. A joint Thai and Danish expedition visited the cave in 1960, and found the remains of four Dong Son-style drums. They could see that there was much to be learned from Ongbah Cave, despite the fact that it had been ravaged by local farmers collecting bat guano for fertilizer. But they could not mount a proper excavation until 1965, by which time further damage had been done to the site by treasure hunters.

Ongbah was a large cave, measuring more than 100 yards long, and had obviously been an ancient burial place. This implied a settlement nearby, and while the exact whereabouts of the settlement itself remained unknown, it was a fortuitous location—between two rivers, in a pass through the mountains (that form the present-day boundary between Thailand and Burma) to the western seacoast, and near a deposit of lead ore. In the few parts of the cave that had remained undisturbed, excavators found two types of burials: Some bodies had been buried in boat-shaped wooden coffins and others had been buried without enclosure.

The researchers concluded that the coffins had been reserved for those of the highest status, with the other burials being of a second high-ranking class. In both types of burials the bodies were accompanied by an assortment of iron implements, and occasionally by a bronze artifact. And the archaeologists discovered that some of the bodies had been adorned with glass beads that could have come only from India, by way of some trade route. The material that could be dated had originated in the second half of the first millennium BC—the same period that had seen the explosion of technology among the distant Dong Son people.

Something important had happened around 500 BC, something unrelated to any foreign incursion or, apparently, isolated to any particular Southeast Asian culture. Whatever had occurred had lent sharp impetus to the region's technology and artistry, especially as expressed in bronze, iron, and—as shown in Ban Chiang's middle-period wares—ceramics. An important clue about what those events had been came from—once again—an unusual source.

In the late 1940s, Peter Williams-Hunt, a British army photographic interpreter with an interest in archaeology, noticed some anomalies in certain aerial photographs taken of the Khorat Plateau during World War II. The anomalies were dark rings of vegetation, enclosing areas that ranged from about 50 acres up to 175 acres, scattered across the Mun River basin of northeastern Thailand. It turned out that the dark rings, almost indistinguishable to people on the

A Han-style brick tomb (left, above)—one of 27 excavated by Olov Janse in the 1930s—lies exposed in northern Vietnam near the coastal village of Lach Truong. The Han, who vanquished the Dong Son people in 111 BC, constructed hundreds of such tombs—which they covered with large earth mounds—as homes for their elite dead. The bronze figurine at left, from such a tomb, displays Vietnamese influence but was modeled after a Chinese funerary lamp. A wick is believed to have poked from the top of the head, soaking up oil pooled in the statuette.

ground, were defined by dense vegetation growing on the crests of ancient earthworks that once surrounded villages or towns.

Eventually, researchers identified in the aerial photographs 91 of these sites, many of which may have flourished in the middle of the first millennium BC. The earthworks—as much by-products of digging moats and other waterworks as they were defensive walls—established one thing beyond argument: These organized villages and substantial public works could have been created only by an organized agrarian society. The improvements had begun, most probably, as simple earthen dikes intended to help retain water in the rice fields surrounding the village. Over time, as the people noted causes and effects, their community projects became ever more complex systems of dams, moats, reservoirs, and canals.

Important implications about the nature of the society arise directly from the amount of time and energy involved in mounting such ambitious projects. If the moats around one of these sites, called Ban Chiang Hian, were just three feet deep, their excavation could have involved the removal of 100,000 cubic yards of earth, a job that would have taken about 500 people a year to complete. Such a task could not have been accomplished without considerable planning and cooperation, with the workers probably toiling at agriculture during the wet season and digging the moat during the dry season.

After a careful survey of the moated sites in the Chao Phraya Valley, researcher C. M. Ho discerned in 1984 that the pattern of their distribution had changed over time. As the metal age progressed, some sites became larger than their neighbors, suggesting an increase in centralized political authority. Eventually, she found the largest sites at intervals of about 18 miles at the time of widespread bronze use and the beginnings of iron use. Thus, the moat builders of central and northeastern Thailand, the boat-coffin makers of western Thailand, and the drum smiths of Vietnam and Yunnan were experiencing their greatest vigor in the middle of the first millennium BC.

Just as it had become clear that major advances had taken place in northern Vietnam before the Chinese arrived, so new evidence from Burma has shown that a great deal had been happening there before the advent of the Indians. And developments in Burma revealed still more connections with the Dong Son drums.

That Burma had been the site of a sophisticated Buddhist cul-

RINGS SEEN FROM ON HIGH

After a long and careful search of British Museum archives in 1982, Elizabeth Moore, an American archaeologist specializing in Southeast Asia, came upon 55 cardboard boxes stuffed with more than 5,000 aerial views of Southeast Asia taken between 1945 and 1950. The collection had been amassed by Major Peter Williams-Hunt *(below)* who was a British army photographic interpreter for an aerial survey of Southeast Asia during World War II. His interest piqued by concentric rings of vegetation that showed up in many shots, some made by him, he focused on the rings; they turned out to mark sites of prehistoric moated villages in northeast Thailand.

By 1949 the major had been posted to Malaysia, where he married the daughter of a Semai Senoi chief. Silverfish and hu-

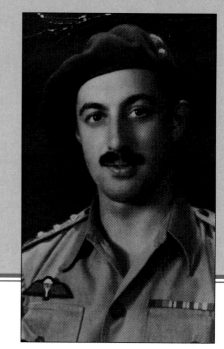

midity were destroying his archives, so he sent them to a London friend, planning to "call in a few years' time." But he died in 1953 when a rotting log gave way, impaling him on a bamboo stake. He was buried according to Semai Senoi custom. Bread, a *panang* (knife), a hatchet, and a blowpipe were put in his grave, with his tweed suit, dress shirt, tie, toilet articles, cigarettes, and an issue of *National Geographic.*

Some 30 years later, Moore painstakingly analyzed thousands of Williams-Hunt's photos, launching her own survey of moated sites in northeast Thailand, which eventually developed into a comprehensive study of Southeast Asian prehistoric water management. The 1994 shuttle *Endeavor's* earth-imaging radar views of Angkor have recently provided Moore with an even more exciting perspective on her work, showing traces of ancient Angkor and its early hydraulic systems.

ture by the fifth century AD, as evidenced by the remains of the monumental city of Sri Ksetra, had been well known by the 1950s. Bearing the clear imprint of Indian religion and culture, such remains seemed to support conventional assumptions about the external forces that presumably had shaped Southeast Asian culture. But according to a leading Burmese archaeologist of the time, U Aung Thaw, prior to 1959 the investigation of the origins of such cities had been only "sporadic." While a great deal of information had been collected about the individual cities, he wrote in 1966, "no attempt has yet been made to correlate these results so as to obtain a chronological sequence of the different phases of early cultures in Burma."

The ruins of the sizable walled city of Beikthano seemed to offer Burmese scientists a chance to take a fresh, more controlled approach to a relatively undisturbed site. Aung Thaw wrote that he and his colleagues set out to obtain, among other information, a fixed point in time "from which to initiate a systematic culture sequence."

The city had been a substantial one; the rectangle formed by its outer brick walls enclosed an area of nearly four square miles. Millennia of erosion had obliterated an entire side of the enclosure and had reduced the other three to about six feet in height. Inside the walls, in addition to a central palace area of about four acres, there were nearly 100 low mounds of debris covered by brush. Outside the walls, surveyors found an expanse of low mounds that proved to be cemeteries in which the citizens had buried their dead after cremation, placing the ashes in terra-cotta urns. Excavations at 25 locales throughout the Beikthano complex took four years to accomplish. The results pushed knowledge of Burmese prehistory some 400 years further into the past, and once again focused on the power and the connectedness of events in Southeast Asia around 500 BC.

The people who thrived in such cities as Sri Ksetra in the middle of the first millennium AD had antecedents living in places such as Beikthano 1,000 years earlier. They became known as the Pyu; they most likely had migrated from the north, from western China, whence they had for some reason been displaced. During the first millennium BC they had moved southward into Yunnan, where they must have had close contact with such bronzeworkers and drum makers as those who lived around Lake Dian. At mid-millennium, they reached what is now Burma, where they apparently established overland contacts with India's border centers to the west, China to the northeast, and the maritime peoples to the south.

Evidence showed that: The Pyu of Beikthano were contemporaries of the Lake Dian and Dong Son peoples; they were primarily farmers who learned to irrigate their fields to survive in the Burmese dry zone; and they may have had some connections to Dian and Dong Son peoples, as suggested by clay objects reminiscent of Dong Son drums. While the drums were similar in shape, decoration, and apparent use to those of the other two cultures, suggesting earlier contact during the Pyu migration, there was an important difference; the Pyu did not work in bronze. Instead, they made elaborate, drumlike vessels of terra cotta. Apparently, the Pyu had no ready source of the ores needed for bronze, and they were perhaps isolated from the maritime routes along which the bronze drums moved.

Anthropological evidence gleaned from studies of surviving, modern drum-using ethnic groups—the Karen in Burma and the Lamet of nearby Laos—suggests the prominent role the drum occupied in some ancient Southeast Asian societies. A proverb survives among the Lamet people: "He who has no drum is unable to call his ancestors." And the intervention of the ancestors was vital to main-

GIANT URNS OF A VANISHED PEOPLE

In the Laotian uplands, dozens of huge stone urns stand in and on the ground. Westerners who beheld them dotting the landscape long wondered about their origin. The locals believed that they were the work of a race of giants, who had used them to hold grain and alcohol. Then, in 1931, French archaeologist Madeleine Colani and her sister arrived on the so-called Plain of Jars to investigate the site and solve the mystery.

Overwhelmed by the sheer number of vessels, Colani decided to begin her explorations in a small cave located in the midst of the plain. As luck would have it, she had stumbled on a cremation grotto, filled with quantities of ash and human bone. The jars, she realized, were probably huge funerary urns, in and around which burial gifts of glass and carnelian beads, cowrie shells, bronze bells and bracelets, iron knives, and spears and arrows had been deposited.

Subsequent radiocarbon testing indicated that the site dates between 300 BC and AD 300, which suggests that the urns may have been contemporary with the Dong Son people. The urns' owners are likely to have enjoyed a particular advantage: They may well have controlled the production of salt in the area and traded it widely, over routes running into China, Thailand, and Vietnam. Through such commerce they would have prospered.

In the years since 1931, the jars have dwindled from Colani's count of 250 to about 200. Though the plain was bombed during the French and the U.S. wars in Southeast Asia, only one jar was destroyed. The rest have fallen prey to unethical antiquities dealers. Most disturbing to archaeologists hoping to return to this corner of Laos is the looters' strength and organization. Many believe that only UNESCO's protection can save the Plain of Jars from further depredation.

taining the fertility of the people, their fields, and their animals. An individual without a drum, according to Cambridge University researcher Janice Stargardt, was "adrift and isolated from the mainstream of an existence in which lineages confer identity and beneficient support in all the vital aspects."

Stargardt, who argues that the Pyu were related somehow to contemporary manifestations of the Dian and Dong Son peoples, has stated that "Together, Dian and Dong Son place the Pyu in a broad context of living cultures in the last centuries BC where the drum was a central symbol in a system of belief and ritual concerning the fundamental questions of the human condition: communication with the ancestors, death and the renewal of life for man, plants and animals." And the accumulating evidence from sites in Vietnam, Thailand, Cambodia, and Burma gave weight to the revisionist argument that these living cultures owed little for their progress to China, India, or any other foreign influence. Instead, as Stargardt put it, "the Dong Son culture was merely the last and most brilliant phase of a long, indigenous development of bronzeworking."

A rotund urn dwarfs two others on the Plain of Jars. Carved from soft local stone, the largest jars weigh some 15 tons, stand 8 feet tall, and measure 10 feet in diameter. They may have originally been covered by fitted wooden lids.

The same evidence that diminished the role of outside influences pointed to spontaneous developments in mid-millennium as each of the indigenous civilizations evolved essentially on its own. Before roughly 500 BC, settlements had been of about equal size, and growth had been slow. Most of the known cultures of the region were familiar with bronzeworking, but production of metal artifacts—in terms of size and elaboration of individual pieces—was low. The societies were linked by extensive trade networks—along the Chao Phraya, Red, and Mekong Rivers, for example, and the Vietnam coast—through which they exchanged stone, shell, and metal.

Possession of these valuables perhaps conferred status and inspired acquisitiveness. As demand for various items increased, so of course did competitiveness, and certain villages discovered that they had an edge. Perhaps their people occupied better land than their neighbors and were thus able to produce surpluses and make them available for trade; perhaps they controlled a mountain pass, a river crossing, or the source of a specific raw material or trade item.

The basis of subsistence before the first millennium BC was rice. Its production required finding and claiming the marshy bottomland where rice grew naturally, clearing the land during the dry season by felling trees, grubbing out weeds with hoes, and burning straw so that the rice would flourish during the rainy season. Such a system of production was limited by the amount of suitably wet, flat, and fertile land that could be found and cultivated by manual labor.

But during the first millennium BC the equation was changed dramatically by the application of animal power to wet-rice cultivation. Using a water buffalo to draw a plow through the rice field not only increased the area that one person could bring under cultivation but also increased the fertility of the soil by aerating it and returning to it the organic material of the turned-under plants. Moreover, with a water buffalo one could build small earthen dikes to retain water on soil previously too well drained to support rice.

The larger harvests that followed the advent of the buffalo-drawn plow may have supported increases in population or a change in the concentration of population. Associated changes in trading patterns, in social rank, and in economic specialization among the communities may have occurred so that the powerful or more affluent communities came to have influence over their less-productive or more isolated and dispersed neighbors. Increased population densities may have encouraged more overt displays of rank differences in

In an age-old scene, a Southeast Asian farmer uses a water buffalo to plow a paddy on the edge of a Thai village just as his ancestors did in the first millennium BC, when such animals came to be used in rice cultivation. This shift may well have given rise to food surpluses that helped bring about larger populations.

feasts and rituals, which in turn created yet more demand for crafted articles, such as Dong Son drums for group ideological activities. While no archaeological evidence demonstrates the shift in the organization of bronze production for this period in areas producing the large bronze drums, it seems possible that in north Vietnam the economic role of bronzeworkers evolved from small-scale individual producers to larger scale operations, probably patronized by the elite.

Such developments could have had an ever-widening and profound impact. Social organization changed; large, politically centralized settlements, perhaps ruled by regional chieftains, replaced the autonomous settlements upon which society had previously been based. Technology changed; smiths began to work with iron. Commerce changed; trade items from India and China began to appear among burial belongings late in the first millennium BC. And as significant as these advances were for the dwellers on the mainland and nearby islands of Southeast Asia, the latter influence—the impulse to travel in search of resources and new lands—had unsuspected implications for a substantial portion of the planet.

Evidence for vibrant late Stone Age cultures in Southeast Asia had come from many nontraditional, nonarchaeological sources. Among these were botanists, who made a major contribution by tracing the origins of domesticated plants as indigenous to the region. And linguists cast a new light on the earliest peoples of the area.

Bearing spirals, scrolling ribbons, concentric circles, and other artistic motifs similar to those found on Dong Son drums, this cast-bronze ceremonial ax was unearthed along with two others on the small Indonesian island of Roti in 1875. The ax, which measures more than 30 inches long, may have been made sometime during the first millennium AD by local metalworkers whose forebears had been influenced by contact with the Dong Son culture.

The words that people invent, modify, and preserve offer indirect but valid evidence about their lives and history. Analysis of the word usage of the inhabitants of Southeast Asia can be bewildering at first, since more than 1,000 distinct and mutually unintelligible languages are in use. But analysis of word use and structure reveals affinities among tongues and makes possible their categorization in related families with common ancestors. Nearly 50 percent of the world's population, including India's, speaks languages classified as Indo-European, descended from a prototype that probably originated in west-central Russia. But despite the prominence of Indian influence in the architecture, literature, and religion of historic Southeast Asia, none of the region's languages has an Indo-European base.

Most of the tongues can be grouped into four linguistic families. The Sino-Tibetan family includes the dialects common to Burma. Thai and Lao are found mostly in the Chao Phraya and the Kong Valleys in Laos and Thailand. The third major language family of mainland Southeast Asia is Austroasiatic, and includes Vietnamese and Khmer, which is spoken today mainly in Cambodia, with pockets in nearby Thailand and Vietnam. The prehistoric residents of Non Nok Tha and Ban Chiang probably spoke an ancestral version of Austroasiatic. The fourth language family, Austronesian, is in many respects the most remarkable, for the number of languages it embraces and for the extent of its spread.

Austronesian stretches a third of the way around the globe, from Madagascar to Easter Island, and includes the national languages of Malaysia, Indonesia, and the Philippines, as well as hundreds of regional and minority tongues in these three countries and in the South Pacific islands. The Austronesian family encompasses nearly 1,000 languages, probably more than any other language family. All Austronesian languages derive from a single language called Proto-Austronesian, which linguists believe was spoken on Taiwan when, sometime after 4000 BC, it began to spread south to the Philippines and Borneo, west to Java, Sumatra, and the Malay Peninsula, and finallly east to the Pacific islands and west to Madagascar.

Linguists have confirmed that the Austronesian speakers had in their vocabulary words that revealed much about those who used the various languages. Words for such implements as paddles, sails, and outrigger floats implied that the people possessed the highly seaworthy outrigger canoe. They spoke of rice, and of more than one variety of millet, in ways that suggest they were cereal farmers. In-

deed, it has recently been postulated that only farmers, with their food surpluses and higher population densities, could sustain a major migration and colonization effort. According to linguists such as Robert Blust of the University of Hawaii, the ancient Taiwanese lived in substantial houses built atop pilings, wove their own cloth, were familiar with some metals, hunted with bows and arrows, and cared for domestic water buffalo, pigs, and dogs.

The linguists deduced from their evidence something that flew in the face of another piece of conventional wisdom but helped archaeologists account for anomalies often encountered in digs; the concept of culture loss. After the Austronesian speakers had moved offshore and had settled their lush islands, their language indicates

Part of the eighth-century-AD Buddhist Javanese monument of Borobudur, this volcanic rock panel depicts a sailing ship and its passengers being greeted on land by people who may live in the house on stilts seen in the background. Far-ranging Southeast Asian sailors established trading routes to India, Asia, the Pacific, and the east coast of Africa in similar vessels, which were equipped with outriggers and multiple sails.

that as the centuries passed they forgot about things they had learned to do over generations, but that were no longer needed or possible. Some groups eventually had no rice agriculture, big houses, weaving, domesticated animals, metallurgy, or pottery.

Thus, researchers who probe only recent prehistory, and find people who possess no particularly advanced cultural skills, may mistake their line of inquiry for a blind alley. Until linguists discovered what the inhabitants of the Pacific islands had forgotten, and the University of Hawaii's seafaring anthropologist Ben Finney demonstrated what their ancestors could have accomplished with their voyaging canoes, archaeologists could not fully explain how or by whom the islands of the South Pacific had been settled.

It is now widely accepted that the most important agents of the migration were blue-water sailors from the southeast coast of Vietnam, Malaysia, Indonesia, and the Philippines. They reached as far as the east coast of Africa by the first century BC. They eventually established regular trade routes to India, the Red Sea, and the South Pacific islands, which they progressively settled and colonized.

According to Finney, "this spread of Austronesian speakers throughout island and coastal Southeast Asia to Madagascar and almost clear across the Pacific made the Austronesian language family the most widespread one in the world—until Western Europeans developed their own seafaring technology and carried Indo-European tongues around the globe." It was a remarkable diaspora indeed, involving the spread of ancient peoples across a watery region equivalent in size to Europe and much of Asia combined.

At least one scholar, while trying to gather the many strands of Southeast Asian history into a coherent pattern, glimpsed an even more spectacular possibility. Lynda Shaffer of Tufts University proposed that the double-canoe voyagers who settled Polynesia were the agents of a process analogous to what is known as "westernization," which means the spread of cultural and technological advances from Western Europe. But Shaffer sees in the emerging evidence signs of a process that occurred before the westernization of recent times, which she labels "southernization," and by which she means the spread of cultural and technological advances indigenous to southern Asia, including the Indian subcontinent and greater Southeast Asia—in metallurgy, medicine, agriculture, textiles, and trade—not only to China and Africa but to the Middle East and beyond.

In other words, from about AD 1 to 1500, southern Asia was the focus of the global economy and of the world's most dynamic ideologies and religions. Not until European societies, through technological innovation and economic change, were able to take over the southern-based spice trade, did the center of the global economy shift from the southern Asian seas to the North Atlantic.

Whether or not Shaffer's concept of southernization will ever be widely accepted, little doubt remains that by the first century AD the peoples of Southeast Asia had, all by themselves, reached highly sophisticated levels of cultural and technological attainment. These peoples were prepared for another transformation, but this time they were becoming players in a larger scenario, as the economy of the world was becoming increasingly globalized.

For 19th-century romantics, the jungle-covered, abandoned cities of Southeast Asia exerted a strong pull. One man to respond to the region's lure was Henri Mouhot, a young French naturalist, who risked health and family fortune in 1858 to set off—with the blessings of England's Royal Geographical Society—on a journey of exploration. After being feted by the king of Cambodia, he met a group of French missionaries, one of whom led him to the vast Khmer complex of temples known as Angkor, with its walled city of Angkor Thom.

These exotic structures entangled in vines and roots had previously been described by a Chinese diplomat, Portuguese and Spanish travelers, and French missionaries. But their words had little effect in the West, perhaps because most of the public lacked the means to visualize Angkor's mysterious beauty. It was Mouhot who rectified this situation by sketching what he saw.

The intrepid 35-year-old went on to explore Laos,

where he succumbed to a fever in 1861. His jou[rnal] with his evocative sketches and vivid descriptions[,] sent to his wife, who had it published in 1863 a[nd] with a series of engravings made by French pri[nters] from his drawings. While his account made no clai[m to] his having "discovered" Angkor, that credit wa[s ac]corded him by a press and public eager for a new [hero.]

Inspired by Mouhot and the artists who follo[wed] him, travelers trekked to the Cambodian tem[ples,] among them three unknown French tourists and [their] guide, whose picture *(above)* was taken by an an[ony]mous photographer in the 1890s as they posed on [one] of Angkor's many small temples. Such images [also] spurred the French colonial spirit then on the rise: [the] early Khmer kings had built the spired temples to p[lease] the gods and glorify themselves; soon the new E[uro]pean rulers of Cambodia would begin to restore t[hem] as a way of asserting their own legitimacy in the [land] that was to become known as French Indochina.

67

An engraving made from a water-
color Mouhot sent to his family shortly
before he died shows him sketching in
the jungle (left) with elephants nearby.
Mouhot reported an encounter with
a herd of the animals en route to Angkor: The leader, "a male of enormous
size" greeted his approach with a
"frightful" roar. But at the sound of
a gunshot, "the herd stopped in astonishment," then marched away.

Below, a gallery extends from Angkor
Wat's central portico; in the fore-
ground Mouhot has drawn a heron.
The main entrance (left) is reached by
crossing the surrounding moat over a
causeway more than 1,000 feet long
and 30 feet wide. A balustrade (lower
left), raised on stone pillars, is carved
in the form of a Naga, a mythological
beast with the body of a snake.

Six French explorers were sent to determine the navigability of the Mekong River shortly after Cambodia became a French protectorate in 1864. Among the explorers was Louis Delaporte, a naval officer skilled at cartography, who gave the mission an additional goal—the acquisition for France of Khmer art.

After a second trip to Cambodia in 1873, Delaporte returned to France with more than 70 sculptural and architectural fragments. Later, they would become the core collection of a new Indochinese museum under his direction. He also brought back a number of casts of Angkor's architectural details, using them to create models that showed the Khmer style without replicating actual buildings.

Multiple faces of King Jayavarman VII—13th-century builder of much of Angkor who had himself portrayed here as a Bodhisattva, or "Enlightened Being"—greet visitors entering the southern gateway of his royal city of Angkor Thom (above). *Elephant traffic on the causeways and terraces of the western approach of Angkor Wat is seen in the panorama below; Delaporte has included himself drawing.*

Enormous sculptures from another Khmer religious center, the great Preah Khan temple, some 60 miles east of Angkor, float through the jungle (right), bound for France. Similar rafts are believed to have been used centuries earlier—during the construction of Angkor's temples—for transporting millions of tons of sandstone from a quarry approximately 25 miles to the northeast. Some of the many statues taken by the French from the Preah Khan temple and other monuments were lost en route when rafts capsized.

FINDING THE HIDDEN MEANING

Although Europeans came to admire the Khmer temples, they were at first puzzled by the unusual architecture. But scholars and architects—including Lucien Fournereau, who made these drawings—soon concluded that the moats, terraces, and towers were meant to stand for the continents, mountains, and oceans of the Hindu universe.

In the 1860s, Fournereau had been an explorer in Guiana, South America. Inspired by the accomplishments of Delaporte, in 1887 he traveled to Angkor, where he sketched, took pho-

tographs, and made more than 500 casts of parts of temples. Some of his ink-and-watercolor drawings were in the romantic vein that had characterized the work of his predecessors, but he also produced meticulous plans, cross sections, and elevations of the buildings. These remained unsurpassed in scope and accuracy for the next 70-odd years.

When Fournereau returned to Paris, he displayed his images at the Salon, an important annual French exhibition. Fournereau's work helped bring about an appreciation of Khmer genius.

Two monks meditate near the so-called Terrace of the Leper King, named for the statue of a nude male on the right. Once believed to be an image of Jaya-varman VII (according to one Khmer legend, the king contracted leprosy from an admiring subject's impulsive kiss), the sculpture is today thought to depict a god.

These two Fournereau drawings of the 11th-century Baphuon temple in Angkor Thom show the whole monument and an east-west elevation. The simplicity and symmetry of the reconstruction at upper right reflects the vision of such a temple as a cosmic mountain. The lower view reveals that the Baphuon, like other temples in the area, was built atop a rise on which earth was heaped. The loose-soil underpinning caused the building—one of Angkor's greatest monuments—to collapse.

ETAT ACTUEL

COUPE LONGITUDINALE EST OUEST

When the photographer and colonial Leon Busy arrived in Angkor in 1921 to take pictures, the clearing and conserving of the complex had been under way since 1907. He had been commissioned by French banker and philanthropist Albert Kahn to take autochromes, the first color photographs, as part of an ambitious, worldwide project designated Archives of the Planet. His images beautifully captured the poetic moodiness of the sites, many of which are still in use.

Angkor had changed considerably since Mouhot's day. Visitors were now accommodated in bungalows. Still smitten with Mouhot's image of vegetation-smothered monuments, many resented attempts to cut back the encroaching plants. To placate the dissenters, the French left a few structures untouched, designated as "conservation" areas. Toward the end of the 20th century, after decades of warfare, the jungle reestablished its stranglehold on the temples, returning Angkor almost to the state in which it existed when Mouhot first beheld it.

Evidence of continuing worship, offerings covered in red cloth—the favorite color of spirits—have been placed before the sculpture seen below. The piece stands in the ruined brick tower of Bakheng, the earliest temple constructed in Angkor. Busy's autochromes, the first photographs of Angkor in color, took 30 times as long to make as black-and-white pictures.

A still-venerated eight-armed statue of the Hindu god Vishnu (above), *more than 10 feet high, stands in the galleries of Angkor Wat's western entrance. Vishnu was absorbed into Khmer tradition, becoming a local divinity called Neak Ta Moha Reach.*

ARCHITECTURE IN SERVICE OF KINGS AND GODS

It had been a long journey—almost 200 miles by elephant from Bangkok in Siam into the central plain of neighboring Cambodia. But to the British governess Anna Harriette Leonowens and her companions, who made the trek in 1865, the hardship and the perils of travel paled amid the romance of the exotic world through which they passed. "The rainbow mists of morning still lay low on the plain," Leonowens recalled, "as yet unlifted by the breeze that, laden with odor and song, gently rocked the higher branches in the forest, as our elephants pressed on, heavily but almost noiselessly, over a particolored carpet of wild flowers."

Such enthusiasm characterized its writer, for Anna Leonowens was a remarkable figure. In an age when most women were confined to roles in the home, the unlikely explorer enjoyed an unorthodox career. When her husband, a major serving in the British army in Asia, had died in 1858, the 24-year-old widow decided to stay on in Singapore. Four years later, an invitation from King Mongkut of Siam took her to the royal palace in Bangkok. There Leonowens served as tutor to the king's children, later publishing her experiences in *An English Governess at the Siamese Court*. In the 20th century, her story inspired books, movies, TV series, and perhaps most memorable, the Rodgers and Hammerstein musical *The King and I*.

Now the governess had been enticed into the jungles of the

Mythical monkey kings fight viciously in a relief on the Banteay Srei temple complex 10 miles north of Angkor. Considered a masterpiece of 10th-century-AD architecture, the reliefs were inspired by Hindu legends brought to the area by Indian Brahmins and traders.

central Cambodian plain. Two years earlier, the publication of the journal of the French naturalist Henri Mouhot had alerted Europeans to the existence of ruins amid the vegetation. Leonowens's journey took her from Siam—or Thailand—east across the Dangrek Mountains into the interior of Cambodia, a vast basin barely six feet above sea level through which the Mekong River flows on its journey to the South China Sea. Northeast of the Tonle Sap—the freshwater lake that dominates the heart of the plain—lie dense forest and jungle, where tall fromager trees and gray-white giant figs, covered

The rising sun burns away the morning mist to outline the towers of Angkor Wat and an enormous carved-stone Naga. Borrowed from Indian mythology, the multiheaded serpent became a favorite motif of Khmer architects and is seen here forming the balustrade of the main causeway at Angkor Wat. Similarly, the lion—much represented in Indian and Chinese art of the period—also received great play in the hands of the Khmer; one guards the entrance to the causeway.

with lichen and shrouded in creepers, filter the sunlight to a soft, green glow. It was here that Leonowens reached her goal.

Before the governess stood an entire city swallowed up by the jungle, the works of man in a struggle with the works of nature. The vegetation seemed to enhance the magnificence of it all: Piles of stones rose up in great towers; trees sprouted through cracks in the masonry; carvings covered the walls of the ruins; and from behind thick, tangled roots, giant carved faces peered at her. This was Angkor, the lost capital of ancient Cambodia.

Among all the ruins at the site, one stood out above the rest: Angkor Wat, literally, the "Temple of Angkor." To get to the temple, Leonowens and her party made their way along a causeway that crossed a moat. The causeway, wide enough for 20 people to walk abreast, was lined with stone railings whose ends reared up in the shape of a multiheaded cobra. Passing through a gate in the temple's outer walls, they entered the temple's inner precinct. "We wandered in astonishment, and almost with awe," Leonowens wrote, "through labyrinths of courts, cloisters, and chambers, encountering at every turn some new marvel, unheard of, undreamed of, until then." Above everything rose three huge stepped terraces: On the top terrace five conical towers reached skyward like sprouting lotus buds, as though the stone were bursting into life.

Of the skill of the monument's builders there was no doubt. The stones, as smooth as polished marble, were laid without mortar but had been so carefully carved that the joins were hard to find. Also, every pillar and wall was decorated with carvings so that, wrote Leonowens, "the whole temple seems hung with petrified tapestry." But who these craftsmen were remained a mystery. This was, declared Leonowens, "the work of a race of whose existence Western nations know nothing, who have no names in history, yet who builded in a style surpassing the best works of the modern world—stupendous, beautiful, enduring."

Local accounts of how Angkor had been built were as plentiful as they were far-fetched. One old Cambodian had told the naturalist Mouhot that the city had been set "deep in the jungle where the angry gods had hid it from man." Another claimed that Angkor was the work of giants, who had raised the city in a single day. Yet a third informed the Frenchman that it was the creation of a great king who had offended the gods and was turned into a leper; the king's affliction had led to the downfall of the city.

Early European explanations of Angkor were only slightly less fanciful. Modern Cambodians, they concluded, were so primitive that they could surely not be from the same people who had created such a masterpiece. Westerners must have been its builders. "A person versed in the study of letters might suppose it was the work of Trajan," the great Roman emperor, speculated one visiting 17th-century Spanish missionary. "But although this latter extended his empire farther than all his predecessors, I have never heard that he ever arrived as far as Cambodia." Alexander the Great, however, had come farther east than the Romans and another report attributed the city's construction to him. Only after Mouhot's rediscovery of the site in 1860 did the real history of Angkor begin to unfold.

To piece together the city's past, scholars turned to evidence from three sources: the archaeological and sculptural records, the inscriptions that adorned Angkor's monuments, and contemporary accounts made by foreign visitors. All three would confirm that this had been the heart of the once-great civilization of the Khmers, from whom the inhabitants of today's Cambodia had descended.

For half a millennium—beginning in the late eighth century—the people who erected Angkor ruled over an empire that included much of mainland Southeast Asia. One of the places visited by Anna Leonowens was Angkor Thom—or the "Great City"—the last in a succession of Khmer capitals that stood near the Tonle Sap. Modeled on the perfection of heaven and ruled by kings who were themselves godlike in their status, Angkor was a divine city on earth. Eschewing the perishable wood and thatch from which they built human dwellings, the Khmers had raised enduring temples in stone; the inscriptions they carved on the buildings proclaimed the link between the gods and their own earthly rulers.

But the gods worshiped by the Khmer people had origins far from Cambodia. The capital's moated, stepped monuments—known as temple mountains—represented Mount Meru, the traditional home of the Hindu gods of India. One of these deities, Shiva, the omniscient creator, emerged as the inspiration for most of the god-kings who reigned over Angkor. Even the name Angkor came from a word meaning "city" in Sanskrit, the sacred language of Hinduism.

This photograph taken in the 1920s inside a gallery at Angkor Wat shows some of the stunning interior architecture, carvings, and freestanding sculpture that delighted European visitors of the day. Though Khmer architects never mastered the curved arch, a technique used by Roman and European builders to create vast, vaulted ceilings, they were able to achieve a cathedral-like feeling by using a corbeled, or false, arch. The arch, however, often proved unstable and collapsed.

Indian culture had been moving out from the Asian subcontinent since the beginning of the Christian era, at a time when the benefits of Roman civilization were being disseminated throughout Western Europe. Sailing on the seasonal monsoon winds, Indian mariners bound for China crossed the Bay of Bengal and put ashore in Southeast Asia, staying for months at a time while they waited for the winds to change. Among their passengers were Hindu Brahmins and Buddhist monks, who carried with them not just their faith and the Sanskrit language. With them, too, came a belief in the close links between a cosmic, all-embracing heaven and the earthly world.

It is now known that by the time the first Indian sailors arrived in Southeast Asia, distinct societies had already taken shape there. Far from passively accepting Indian influence, the elites of these societies likely incorporated the new ways, blending them with local practices and traditions to produce cultures of a particularly Southeast Asian type. It has been suggested, for example, that early Cambodians had a theory of "unequal souls" and a belief that the souls of lesser individuals could benefit from the leadership provided by the great souls of their betters. Caste-conscious Hinduism could reinforce such beliefs about the uneven distribution of prowess—and the relationship between rulers and ruled.

Power in Southeast Asia came to depend upon the personal qualities of a leader—and on his ability to attract followers and secure alliances. No border posts or fixed frontiers marked the territories of these leaders; instead, some historians suggest, the land was divided into fluid spheres of influence that have been called *mandalas*. This Sanskrit word describes a political system of touching circles that denote the limits of each ruler's power. As alliances shifted, so some of the circles expanded while others contracted. The ruler of a *mandala* might—through warfare or the forging of coalitions—establish overlordship among neighboring *mandalas*. But such hegemonies, which depended on the prowess of an individual, were generally short-lived, rarely enduring beyond the death of the overlord.

In the constant struggle for enhanced status, overlords turned to the gods for help. Identification with Shiva, in particular, offered what one historian has called a "divine charter for kingship." Such beliefs would underpin the cultures of the region for centuries. Ultimately, however, the demands of serving the gods would come to destroy the very civilizations they had created.

Scholars investigating the rise of the *mandalas* have been particularly interested in the history of the Mekong Delta at the tip of southern Vietnam. It was here that Indian merchants, following the coasts, had to "turn the corner" of Southeast Asia before entering the South China Sea. From about AD 100 the area was dominated by the trading kingdom of Funan. Scholars hypothesize that the Funanese adopted some customs and religious beliefs brought by the seafarers. The enhanced status that came by association with the new ideas, in fact, earned Funan's monarchs the title "Kings of the Mountain," linking them with the Hindu pantheon of Mount Meru. Around 550, however, the Funanese were overthrown by invaders from the north. Power shifted to the plains of Cambodia's interior.

During the sixth century AD, Chinese visitors to central Cambodia spoke of another

linked the city with the bordering Gulf of Thailand and with nearby settlements. Most of Oc Eo's houses and palaces were built of wood, of which few traces remain. But several larger buildings, presumably temples, were constructed of more durable brick and stone.

During his excavations, which were carried out by Vietnamese workers *(left, below)*, Malleret found a wealth of artifacts. Among them were a Chinese Han period mirror and Indian jewelry, including gold rings with Sanskrit seals, finds that established that Oc Eo was a trade center between the two civilizations. Malleret also uncovered evidence of thriving local bronze, jewelry, and pottery industries. And he found items of Mediterranean origin, including second-century-AD Roman coins and the carnelian intaglio above.

Digs in the 1980s and 1990s conducted by the Vietnamese turned up more Indian trade goods, further confirming Oc Eo's links to the rest of Asia.

kingdom. The Chinese called it the state of Zhenla, but modern scholars—reluctant to accept that it was a single political entity—prefer to view Zhenla as a place of shifting, ephemeral *mandalas.* Its rulers are remembered in the inscriptions that grace Zhenla's monuments. "He is like the sun in the sky, radiating an intolerable majesty, the issue of the revered kings of the earth. He was anointed with sacred water, provided blessings, and was foremost among the virtuous." So reads a Sanskrit inscription about one overlord from a city east of the Tonle Sap. Excavations at one site in the middle Mekong Valley uncovered three walled temple precincts, carved with decorative motifs—foliage, fantastic sea monsters, geese—that have parallels in Indian monuments. Inside the precincts were brick-and-stone sanctuaries that held the linga, a stylized stone phallus that represented the life-giving power of Shiva.

In time, the overlords who built these sanctuaries came to declare their godlike status in even more explicit terms. Subtle changes in the formulaic temple inscriptions indicate that between the sixth and eighth centuries ever more powerful rulers emerged in Zhenla. One inscription went so far as to describe a Zhenla king as "an incarnate portion of the god."

Indian ideas began to spread across the indefinite boundaries of the *mandalas.* East of Zhenla, for example, in what is now central Vietnam, the rulers of Champa also adopted the cult of Shiva. The Cham were a farming and trading people who settled some 2,000 years ago on the long coast of the South China Sea and in the narrow, remote valleys of the hinterland. An atlas published in 1902, which still left much of the area blank, dismissed it as a "little-known and very mountainous region."

As with Zhenla, contemporary Chinese records portrayed Champa as a coherent kingdom. The description is again misleading. Scraps of information furnished by Cham inscriptions and archaeological evidence point to a different kind of society. Mountains and inaccessible terrain shaped Cham settlement into small, scattered communities that one scholar has described as an inland archipelago. In these communities—each of which was largely cut off from the others—ambitious overlords established a number of ever-changing centers of authority.

A cult of divine kingship buttressed the power of these Cham overlords, too. In the north of their territory, set in a valley among deep-green mountains, lies Mi Son, Champa's sacred center from the

83

His expression appropriately fierce, this sword-wielding guardian, wearing three-headed Naga ornaments and an elaborate headdress, once ornamented the ninth-century-AD Cham Buddhist monastery at Dong Duong, Vietnam. He stands on a water buffalo while a warrior, who appears tiny in comparison, faces him.

seventh to the 10th centuries AD. An hour's hike across rough terrain from the nearest modern road, the remote site still holds 10 of the 70 brick temples that once stood there in declaration of the power of the king. The windowless structures were built around a square inner sanctum that housed the linga of Shiva *(pages 122-123)*.

But unlike those of Zhenla, Champa's temples boast lavish, carved ornamentation—porticoes, arches, and tiered roofs—in which curves and scrolls are prominent *(page 110)*. Such differences attest to the evolution of a style distinct from that of Champa's neighbors to the west. For this was a region not simply subject to the customs of India, filtered through Zhenla. Its long coastline provided an ideal landfall for Indian merchants bound to and from China, who traded Japanese and Chinese silks in return for Cham sandalwood, gold, and slaves. Eventually, cultural influences from India—as well as China and the islands of Indonesia—would come from the sea as freely as did items of trade.

In 1902, Frenchman Henri Parmentier discovered evidence of these influences when he partly excavated a site at Dong Duong, some 20 miles from Mi Son. There he found a large Buddhist temple complex, three courtyards around a central tower, and 18 shrines. All had been enclosed within a brick wall some 330 yards long and 170 yards wide. According to inscriptions at the site, this had been a monastery built by royal order around AD 875. It seemed that elements within Cham society—probably the elite—had absorbed Buddhism as well as Hinduism, the two faiths coexisting peaceably.

Emerging around the fifth century BC from the teachings of an Indian prince called Siddhartha Gautama and known as the Buddha—the "Enlightened One"—Buddhism had originally taught that blessedness, or Nirvana, could be achieved not by worship-

As their ancestors have done for centuries, workers wearing broad-brimmed hats to shield them from the sun cultivate a Vietnamese rice field. An 11th-century Cham temple, its entrance sheathed in vegetation, towers over them. Cham farmers, using the technique known as wet-rice agriculture, produced the grain in such abundance that they were able to trade the surplus to China.

ing gods, but by developing personal morality and renouncing false ideas. But the religion had evolved into various branches that offered Nirvana to a greater number of disciples and into varying forms of ritual expression and belief. Indeed, in some manifestations—such as Mahayana Buddhism's worship of Bodhisattvas, or "Enlightened Beings"—it came to resemble Hinduism's devotion to the gods.

All across Southeast Asia, Buddhism would inspire the raising of astonishing monuments. The ninth-century-AD rulers of the Indonesian island of Java built Borobudur, a mountainous stone structure that served as a representation of Buddhist teachings *(pages 100-101)*. And in central Burma more than 2,000 red-brick temples and monuments still mark the city of Pagan, for 400 years the capital of a people who also dedicated much of their labor and wealth to the service of their faith *(page 105)*.

But the peoples of Southeast Asia would modify the influences that came from India. Stone sculptures at Dong Duong's temple complex, for example, show how Buddhism had evolved from its roots. Art historians believe that the style of the carvings—Buddhas sitting with legs pendant rather than in the more usual cross-legged style, for example—draw on East Asian rather than Indian traditions of representation.

"An art enamored of power rather than classical beauty," says scholar David Snellgrove of the Cham Buddhas, "it may well represent the most astonishing aesthetic experience produced by Buddhism." Buddhism would eventually take root in Cambodia, too. But first a great empire would rise there, inspired by the teachings of Hindu Brahmins, the cult of the god-king, and the imagination of the indigenous people. For to the west of Champa a successor to Zhenla was emerging: the Khmer kingdom of Angkor.

Marveling at the ruins of Angkor in 1865, Anna Leonowens asked herself questions about the city's builders that scholars have since spent more than a century trying to resolve: "What manner of people were these? Whence came their civilization and their culture? And why and whither did they disappear from among the nations of the earth?"

The lead in answering such questions was taken by the French, who by the end of the 19th century controlled the region they called Indochina, today's Vietnam, Laos, and Cambodia. As part of the task of governing their new dominions, the colonial masters established in Hanoi the École Française d'Extrême Orient. Aware of the importance of Angkor, the École dedicated a whole branch of study to the site.

A succession of curators fulfilled their duties at Angkor, clearing the monuments of rubble and vegetation, taking rubbings of inscriptions, making drawings, taking photographs, writing papers, and—as the city's fame grew—giving visitors guided tours of the site. The life demanded dedication in the face of the stubborn jungle, which grew back after every rainy season so that clearance work was never finished. There were other challenges, too. When Jean Commaille, who became curator in 1908, set up his home in a straw hut beside the causeway of Angkor Wat, his wife left him. She claimed that she could not live without her piano. Eight years later, Commaille himself was murdered at the isolated spot.

For almost six decades French archaeologists enjoyed a virtual monopoly on Angkor. The site held few of the common clues, however, from which archaeologists re-create the lives of vanished peoples: no ordinary dwellings or houses, or other signs of settlement; no shops, workshops, or kitchens. Equally scarce are such everyday artifacts as the cooking utensils, weapons, and items of clothing that mark other ancient cities. Instead, there is the evidence offered by the monuments themselves.

To get a picture of this lost civilization, researchers from the École traveled through the jungles of Cambodia to make an inventory of the country's temples. They listed 910 monuments in all, assigning each a number regardless of its size or fame. A small temple at Angkor was dubbed number 486, for example, while Angkor Wat was known simply as number 497. Meanwhile, the École's Georges Coedès spent years comparing photographs of modern Cambodians with faces chiseled onto the walls of Angkor Thom. Discovering physiological resemblances that confounded the view of the Khmers as a lost race, he showed that today's Cambodians are indeed the descendants of the builders of Angkor.

Access to the remote jungle site remained forbiddingly difficult, however, and many scholars preferred to focus their attention on the far more manageable evidence of the Sanskrit and Khmer temple inscriptions. Rubbings of the inscriptions could be taken in the jungle and then studied in the comfort of Paris. This approach was not without its own difficulties, though. The translations and inter-

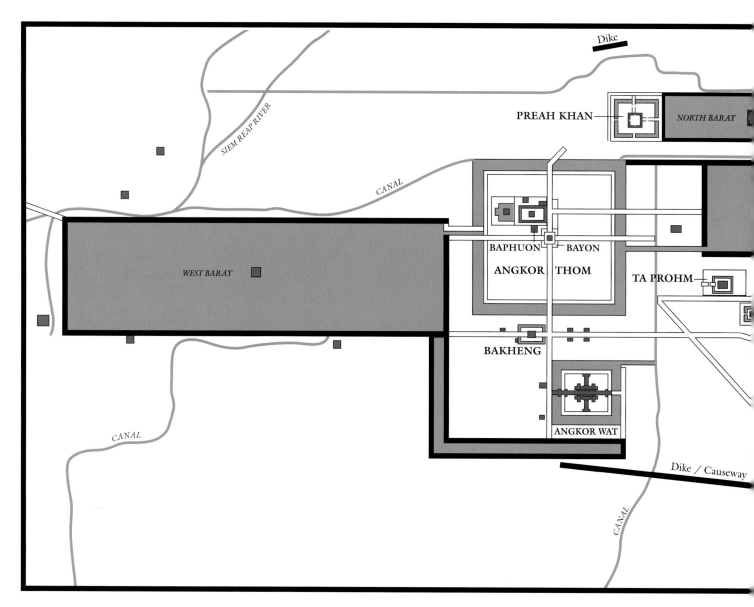

A map based on work done under the auspices of the World Monuments Fund delineates Angkor's network of moats, canals, dikes, and barays (reservoirs). These served multiple purposes, including ritual use, defense, irrigation, drainage, transportation, protein production (fish and waterfowl), and for drinking and bathing. Besides being aesthetically pleasing, the moats around the temples were an effective barrier against white ants, which otherwise would have devoured the religious tomes that were written on palm leaves and kept inside the structures.

pretations encouraged endless debate by epigraphers—specialists in the study of inscriptions—searching for precise meanings. There was also no way to vouchsafe the accuracy of the sources. A ruler who ordered the commission of an inscription was likely less concerned with historical accuracy than in conveying an image of kingship: A claim to have conquered new territory, for example, might reflect a desire to present a mere raid in a glorious light.

But even allowing for royal hyperbole, a historical framework for the Angkorian civilization started to emerge. All of the Khmer kings recorded in the inscriptions added to their name the honorific *varman,* Sanskrit for "protegé of" or "protected by." These formu-

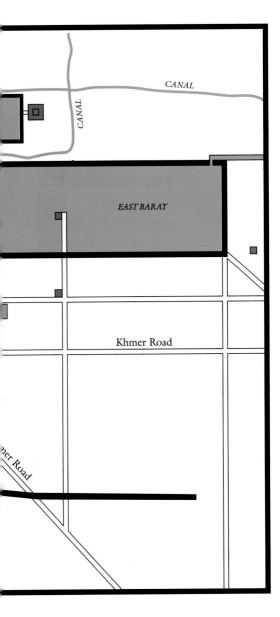

laic names become repetitive, and for clarity Western scholars numbered the various monarchs—who, as a result, sound like Southeast Asian equivalents of William III and Henry VIII. The epigraphic evidence was combined with study of the monuments with which these kings are associated. Among the welter of royal names some individuals began to stand out.

At the beginning of the ninth century AD, a ruler called Jayavarman II—"Protegé of Victory"—rose to prominence over much of what is now Cambodia. Despite war, usurpation, changes of dynasty, and challenges from neighbors, Jayavarman founded a *mandala* that would endure for nearly 500 years.

But like all the rulers and citizens of Angkor, Jayavarman remains a shadowy figure. He is commemorated only in the inscription of Sdok Kak Thom, erected more than 200 years after his death. "Because of this," wrote the great French epigrapher Claude Jacques, "Jayavarman II is probably the Khmer king whose life we know the best—or the least badly." From the scraps of information Jacques has been able to glean from the inscription, scholars have traced a tentative version of the life of this ruler.

It seems that before becoming king, Jayavarman spent many years at the Hindu court of Java, whether as guest, prisoner, or hostage is unclear. His experiences of the Javanese sovereign's lust for conquest may well have fueled Jayavarman's own ambition. Sometime around AD 790, he became one of many rival Khmer rulers vying for power in the lower Mekong plain around the Tonle Sap. Jayavarman managed to subdue many of the neighboring *mandalas* before settling on Mount Kulen, about 25 miles northeast of today's Angkor complex—possibly to escape the enemies he had made among other Cambodian rulers. There, in 802, two years after the coronation in Rome of the great Frankish king Charlemagne, he took a step that would change his 48-year-reign—and Khmer history—forever. The event was later recorded in the Sdok Kak Thom: In a ceremony officiated by a Hindu Brahmin—"learned in the ways of magic"—Jayavarman was pronounced a universal monarch, a god-king, the substance of Shiva.

As a ruler, Jayavarman could demand the allegiance of his people. Now, as a god worthy of worship, he was proclaiming a divine legitimacy over the other rulers of the world. And while he could not have been thinking of the newly crowned Holy Roman Emperor, Jayavarman's action was partly designed to liberate the Khmers from the encroaching influence of Java, where a Buddhist dynasty had pushed out its Hindu neighbors. (A 10th-century Arab writer records that one Javanese ruler had even made his way up the Mekong and beheaded a Khmer leader.) The new Buddhist sovereigns on the island had inherited the Funanese title "Kings of the Mountain." Now Jayavarman was declaring his right to the title.

The site of Jayavarman's elevation reinforced this claim. To drive home the point, he built on Mount Kulen a series of square, single-celled towers with tall, stepped roofs, which recalled Hinduism's heavenly Mount Meru. Centuries of soaking monsoon rains and strangling tree roots have taken their toll on the structures. But these buildings were Cambodia's first temple mountains.

As Jayavarman's power—and self-confidence—grew, he began to move back to the lowlands north of the Tonle Sap. Here he established a new capital city known as Hariharalaya. But the importance of his former highland home was not forgotten. Like the mountain that came to Muhammad, Jayavarman erected on the plains larger versions of the stepped, temple-mountain pyramids that dotted Mount Kulen. Although pyramids had been used earlier in Mesopotamia and Egypt, they had no forebears in India. While following the same Hindu religion, the Cambodians had evolved an architectural form of their own. As Mount Meru stood at the center of the universe, so now the temple mountain would stand at the heart of Hariharalaya and the capitals that succeeded it. And inside the artificial mountain was the sacred linga of Shiva, bearing the name of the sovereign and the god joined as one.

The raising of temples to the gods offered an attractive guarantee of legitimacy for usurpers and sovereigns with tenuous claim to the throne. Each Angkorian ruler built his own monument, which often became his mausoleum after he died. For example, in the year 877, Indravarman was crowned king on the death of Jayavarman II's son. The new monarch was at most Jayavarman's nephew—and possibly not even related to him at all. It was this perhaps insecure ruler who raised the great five-stepped temple mountain known as the Bakong—a "temple exploding stone," as one commentator describes it. To build the Bakong, Indravarman utilized 100 times as much con-

Conceived as a tomb for its builder, Suryavarman II, and as an earthly expression of the Hindu notion of the center
of the universe, the temple of Angkor
Wat rises in a series of terraces toward
the sky. From the summit, some 90 feet
above the ground, visitors gain a magnificent view of the surrounding plain.

struction material as was used for any previous temple. Within it he
placed an image of Jayavarman to honor his supposed ancestor, another way of legitimizing his authority by display.

Just as the supposed mountain home of the Hindu gods was
located north of the Himalayas in a region surrounded by lakes, so
Angkor's major temples were encircled by moats. Adding to what
previous rulers had built, the ambitious Indravarman constructed a
huge reservoir, 150 times bigger than any of those of his predecessors. This water-supply system may have had more than a purely symbolic role. The capital on the plains was well situated. It enjoyed the
benefits of the rich fish stocks of the Tonle Sap, easy river communication, and agricultural land made fertile by regular flooding. But it
also experienced seasonal water shortages, and the reservoirs may also
have been used to combat this problem. Recent research—including
the 1994 use of earth-imaging radar pictures from the space shuttle
Endeavor—is providing additional information about the system.
But just how, and to what extent, irrigation allowed the Khmers to
farm the countryside remains a mystery. Given Angkor's proclivity
for the divine, it is possible that the reservoirs were—like the city's
stone buildings—built purely in honor of the gods.

91

A more unpredictable source of water is mentioned in Angkor's inscriptions. One written about Indravarman by a Hindu guru reads, "As if out of fear of drought, he placed in the heart of all creatures the ambrosia of his charm, which the eyes of women drank insatiably." Males were not excluded, though. The holy man continued: "Upon merely touching the dust of his two lotus feet, men gathered the same fruit they would have acquired by bathing in all the holy pilgrimage sites."

The first king to establish a city on the site of Angkor was Yasovarman, who succeeded Indravarman in AD 889. The construction he began there would continue over the next four centuries—and cover an area the size of Manhattan Island. An inscription crediting him with raising the city's temple mountain was thought to refer to a structure in the middle of Angkor called the Bayon. But the Bayon, scholars later realized, was a Buddhist rather than Hindu monument, and careful stylistic analysis of its carving suggested that it dated from long after Yasovarman's death in the year 900. Yasovarman's true temple mountain was located early in the 1930s by Victor Goloubew, a Russian-born archaeologist of the École Française. Armed with the techniques of aerial photography he had learned during World War I, Goloubew made a painstaking study of maps of the area. He discovered a heap of ruins over a mile south of the Bayon that turned out to be Yasovarman's temple: the Bakheng, or "Mount Mighty Ancestor."

One of Angkor's most remarkable monuments, the Bakheng fuses the creativity of the *mandala*'s sculptors with profound cosmic symbolism. During the 1950s, the meaning of this symbolism was interpreted by the École's Jean Filliozat, a leading authority on Indian cosmology and astronomy. Sitting on a rectangular base, the temple rises in five levels and is crowned by five main towers. Some 104 smaller towers are distributed over the four lower levels, arranged so symmetrically that anyone looking at the monument from the center of any side would see only 33 of them. Thirty-three, Filliozat pointed out, is the number of gods who dwelt on Mount Meru. The Bakheng's total number of towers—109 in all—was also significant. The central tower on the top step, he concluded, represented the axis of the world; the remaining 108 marked the four lunar phases, each with 27 days. The seven levels of the monument symbolize the sev-

POTTERY THAT TRANSCENDS THE MUNDANE

When confronted by the exuberant artistry of the temples at Angkor and the spare design of the period's ceramics, a traveler might well wonder whether the same people created both. The temples' appeal lies in their grandeur, the ceramics' in their modesty. The temples first caught the attention of explorers, who found them sprawling luxuriantly across acres of jungle, their spires and tops soaring out of the trees, made even more romantic by the serpentine vines strangling them. But appreciation of ceramic artifacts was slower in coming. As archaeology of the area increased, so did discovery of pots and jars with graceful and unusual shapes, decorated simply but strikingly. What accounts for the contrast between the buildings and ceramics? The temples were built for the gods; ceramics were made for the people.

Despite the relative plainness of their wares, the potters of Southeast Asia can be called true originals. They combined monochrome glazes with incised patterns or made subtle patterns by employing different colored glazes. For years it was assumed these innovations were introduced by the Chinese. But that theory could not be sustained after the excavation of

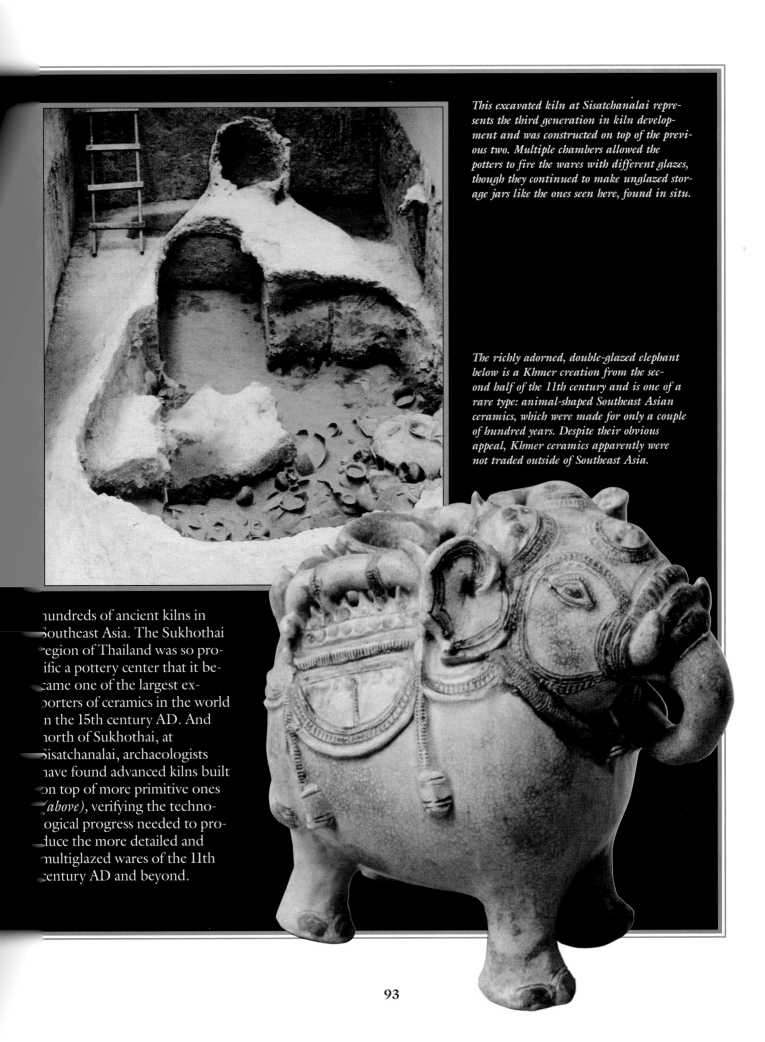

This excavated kiln at Sisatchanalai represents the third generation in kiln development and was constructed on top of the previous two. Multiple chambers allowed the potters to fire the wares with different glazes, though they continued to make unglazed storage jars like the ones seen here, found in situ.

The richly adorned, double-glazed elephant below is a Khmer creation from the second half of the 11th century and is one of a rare type: animal-shaped Southeast Asian ceramics, which were made for only a couple of hundred years. Despite their obvious appeal, Khmer ceramics apparently were not traded outside of Southeast Asia.

hundreds of ancient kilns in Southeast Asia. The Sukhothai region of Thailand was so prolific a pottery center that it became one of the largest exporters of ceramics in the world in the 15th century AD. And north of Sukhothai, at Sisatchanalai, archaeologists have found advanced kilns built on top of more primitive ones *(above)*, verifying the technological progress needed to produce the more detailed and multiglazed wares of the 11th century AD and beyond.

93

en heavens, and each terrace contains 12 towers that signify the 12-year cycle of the planet Jupiter. It is, says University of Chicago scholar Paul Wheatley, "an astronomical calendar in stone."

In the 200 years after Yasovarman, various sons, cousins, and usurpers rose and fell. Then, in AD 1113, Angkor's next great ruler ascended the throne: Suryavarman II, "Protegé of the Sun." Under the new king, the edges of the Angkorian *mandala* were pushed out on many fronts—to the Malay Peninsula in the south, Champa in the east, and Siam in the west, and on to the borders of the Burmese kingdom of Pagan.

"There was once a King Suryavarman," an inscription records, "whose virtue, in imitation of the sun, which made the lotus grow, ensured the constant prospering of each action undertaken." It was in keeping with this conqueror's ambition that he was the one who erected the largest temple mountain. While European masons

As bodies pile up at their feet (bottom row, left), *soldiers of King Jayavarman VII battle the Cham on this sandstone relief decorating the walls of the Bayon at Angkor Thom. War elephants charge across the scene while emboldened Khmer warriors overcome the enemy. The Cham seized Angkor under the rule of Jayavarman's predecessor; in revenge, Jayavarman not only defeated the Cham invaders in his country but pursued the Cham to their homeland and sacked their capital.*

were building that continent's Gothic cathedrals, the sun king Suryavarman was planning the construction of Angkor Wat *(page 91)*.

But Suryavarman faced a problem. By the 12th century the Khmer capital was already crowded with the monuments and canals of earlier kings; no site remained that could hold an edifice worthy of such a king. So Suryavarman raised his temple—his own mortuary shrine—outside the city. Surrounded by a cloistered enclosure measuring some 1,700 by 1,500 feet, the 200-foot-high mountain of Angkor Wat rises in three great terraces. On the uppermost level soar its five cone-shaped towers. Although they have been compared to wings and even pineapples, the towers are, in fact, representations of lotus buds, set in a quincunx arrangement—four at the corners of a square and the largest in the middle.

Construction of Angkor Wat required an enormous quantity of stone, as much as Egypt's great pyramid of Khafre at Giza. One modern engineer has estimated that it would take 300 years to build today. Yet the monument was begun soon after Suryavarman came to the throne, and finished shortly after his death, a period of no more than 40 years. Moreover, virtually all of its surfaces—columns, lintels, even the roofs—are carved. Miles of reliefs illustrate scenes from Indian epic literature and scenes from the legends associated with Suryavarman's chosen deity, Vishnu the Preserver, to whom the temple was dedicated. Fanciful creatures adorn the walls—unicorns, griffins, winged dragons pulling chariots, eagles with peacock tails—as well as warriors, some following an elephant-mounted leader, doing battle with adversaries, demonic as well as human. And everywhere are carvings of Apsaras, sinuous celestial dancing girls with elaborate hair styles and ornate jewelry.

After Anna Leonowens's 200-mile elephant ride, her reaction is understandable. "The majestic ruins of the watt stand like a petrified dream," she wrote, "more impressive in its loneliness, more elegant in its grace, than aught that Greece and Rome have left us." Later visitors have been moved to make similar comparisons. British diplomat Malcolm MacDonald said, "It is the Asian contemporary of Notre Dame de Paris and Chartres Cathedral in France and of Ely and Lincoln Cathedrals in England. But in spaciousness and splendor it is more ambitious than any of these." Another Englishman, author Leigh Williams, wrote that the "stateliest piles of medieval

Europe have paled into insignificance. Spellbound, I watched the sun reveal the immensity of a masterpiece the jungle hid for more than 300 years." But in Angkor Wat the vanity of the Khmers had reached its ultimate expression, its final glory. In the words of French archaeologist Bernard-Philippe Groslier, the Khmers "died of too much glory." For Angkor would perish of its own stone weight.

The massive building projects undertaken by the Khmer kings had placed heavy demands on the population, which toiled unpaid in a system of virtual slave labor. Meanwhile, other duties went unperformed and the economy faltered. Moreover, Suryavarman's military conquests had overextended the empire. In short, while the king strove to reinforce his own status, his kingdom was disintegrating beneath him. The divine union of god and king—deemed essential for the well-being of the empire—was leading to its ruin. When Suryavarman died around 1150, he left a realm exhausted, overstretched, and feeble.

The sun king's death signaled the outbreak of political unrest, and a vulnerable Angkor faced external threats, too. In 1177 the Chams invaded: They sailed up the Mekong, crossed the Tonle Sap, and burned the wooden capital to the ground. The Khmers seemed powerless to resist as their enemy devastated the country. Eventually they rallied under Suryavarman's second cousin, the 50-year-old and Buddhist Jayavarman VII. Not only did the new Khmer leader defeat the Chams on land and in a naval battle fought on the lakes and canals of Cambodia's plains *(pages 94-95)*. He also seized the territory of the aggressors, which became a province of Angkor for the next 20 years. During the reign of this warrior-king, in fact, the borders of an expansionist Khmer empire reached farther than they ever had before.

Angkor Thom, partly built over the old city, was Jayavarman VII's capital. It covered almost four square miles and may have had as many as one million inhabitants, more than any European city at that time. At its core stands

Called "one of the most masterful sculptures of all time," this life-size sandstone statue, found at Angkor Thom, is thought to show Jayavarman VII. Without a biographical inscription to go by, scholars compared the statue's features with known images of the king at the Bayon and were able to tentatively identify the work as a portrait of the king, perhaps even modeled from life. His pious attitude reflects Jayavarman's adoption of the Buddhist religion.

Jayavarman's temple mountain, the Bayon. In rejection of the old Hindu deities that had been unable to protect the city from the Chams—or perhaps to reflect his own religious persuasions—he dedicated his largest temple to neither Shiva nor Vishnu. Angkor's final great monument was raised in honor of Buddha.

The Bayon has been described as a work of sculpture—"a flower of stone"—as much as a piece of architecture. Sitting on a raised stone terrace, its 50 towers—resembling the sprouting lotus-blossom turrets of Angkor Wat—crowd around the monument's central spire. Each tower is carved with four enigmatically smiling faces that gaze out in each of the cardinal directions *(page 116)*. There are 200 faces in all. All those staring eyes can make the Bayon unnerving. The École's Henri Parmentier spent years at Angkor, but never got used to the feeling. "The visitor is oppressed by an evil sensation," he recalled. The French author Pierre Lôti had a similar experience there. "My blood curdled," he wrote. "I was being observed from all sides."

The four faces carved on each tower were long thought to represent the faces of Shiva. But during the 1930s French scholars concluded that the inspiration for the faces more likely came from Buddhism than Hinduism. According to this theory, the faces represent the Bodhisattva Avalokitesvara, a being who has obtained the divine state of Buddhahood but elects to stay on earth to help others find their way to the perfect state of Nirvana. The features of Jayavarman VII himself, the theory holds, stare out as a god-king watching over his people. "He felt the afflictions of his subjects more than his own," an inscription records, "because the suffering of the people constitute the suffering of the king, more than his own suffering."

Around the Bayon, Jayavarman's Angkor Thom is an architectural model of the universe, a city that would last "for as long as the sun and the moon shall endure." Inside an eight-mile moat—said to have been filled with crocodiles—stood the city walls. They were approached by causeways, along both sides of which ran balustrades formed by rows of giant stone figures. Each row held a great nine-headed serpent. The balustrade recalls the creation myth known as "The Churning of the Sea of Milk." According to the tale, gods and demons in a cooperative effort agitated the primeval milk ocean—represented by the city's moat—for 1,000 years. Together they tugged back and forth on the head and the tail of the serpent king Vasuki, who was coiled around Mount Meru. The mountain then acted as a churning stick, and out of the churned sea came all the creatures of the world.

On a more practical level, Jayavarman also built more than 200 rest houses and hospitals throughout the land. And like the emperors of Rome, he maintained a road system that linked his imperial capital with provincial centers. "No other Cambodian king," says the historian Georges Coedès, "can claim to have moved so much stone." But this Buddhist king was to be the last of the great Angkorian builders, and under him the capital reached its final form. For the nature of the *mandala* was changing.

Unlike the elitist Hinduism of previous rulers, Buddhism—which had long been popular with the masses—was a religion in which the people participated fully. The Buddhist Bayon, for example, is the only temple complex in the city without an enclosing wall, and is the only one where the carvings depict scenes of everyday life. Rather than a great mausoleum for a dead sovereign, this may have been a place open to public worship.

Angkor would continue as the Khmer capital for another 150 years. At the end of the 13th century, a Chinese ambassador named Chou Ta-Kuan visited Cambodia. His report reveals some of the city's glory. "When the king leaves his palace," he wrote, "the procession is headed by the soldiery; then come the flags, the banners, the music. Girls of the palace, three or five hundred in number, gaily dressed, with flowers in their hair and tapers in their hands, are massed together in a separate column. The tapers are lighted even in broad daylight." As the parade moved on, the visitor noticed, its extravagance increased. Following shield- and lance-wielding warriors came "chariots drawn by goats and horses, all adorned with gold," and "ministers and princes, mounted on elephants."

Next were the royal wives and concubines "in palanquins and chariots, or mounted on horses or elephants, to whom were assigned at least a hundred parasols mottled with gold." At the end of the procession came the king himself, standing on an elephant whose tusks were encased in gold. The envoy observed, "All around was a bodyguard of elephants, drawn close together, and still more soldiers for complete protection, marching in close order."

Although this account depicts a thriving city, Chou was witnessing the last days of the Khmer empire. Angkor's star had set. Jayavarman VII had been its last great builder, its last great warrior, and the final years of his reign had coincided with the rise of the

THE PUZZLING TREASURES OF WONOBOYO

In October 1990, Mrs. Cipto Suwarno hired some neighbors to dig on land she owned near the village of Wonoboyo in central Java. Her aim was simply to lower the level of the parcel so that she could water it with the flow from a nearby irrigation ditch. Instead, she set in motion one of Indonesia's great archaeological discoveries.

On October 17 the workers uncovered three green ceramic vessels measuring about 12 inches tall. Inside and around them lay a dazzling array of gold and silver objects, weighing 36 pounds and including finger rings, ear pendants, necklaces, bracelets, coins, saucers, water scoops, a spoon, and the gold lotus-inspired bowl seen at right, which may have been used to hold flower petals during rituals. More was to come. On November 26 a container of 6,396 gold coins weighing 33 pounds was unearthed. Yet another cache, over 10 pounds of jewelry and other ornaments, turned up the next February.

Two weeks after the first find, a team of archaeologists came to Wonoboyo to conduct excavations that might shed light on the trove's origins. Digging 100 yards from the first cache revealed the brick foundations of a building, animal bones, and pottery sherds, indicating that the gold had been buried near or in a settlement.

This left unanswered the questions of who buried the gold, and when and why. Short inscriptions in Old Javanese on the bottoms of the bowls and saucers bear two names, but researchers cannot determine whether these belong to one person or two, or to a male or female. A large gold alms bowl was of a type a retired noble might have carried when, forsaking worldly ways, he chose the life of a priest. One scholar has speculated that the riches may have been abandoned as a nearby volcano erupted early in the 10th century AD—a catastrophe that may have caused the Central Javanese Kingdom to end abruptly and another power to spring up in the east. Instead of being deliberately buried, the trove may have been covered by falling ash.

Mongols. Under Genghis Khan these horse-borne warriors overran China, and in 1259, Genghis's grandson Kublai Khan began pushing farther south. He drove out of northern Vietnam the Annamites, who in turn moved farther south and occupied the land of Champa, which had freed itself of Khmer domination in AD 1220. The Thai people of southern China, meanwhile, were migrating into the land that today bears their name. Cambodia now lay directly between two aggressive nations, the Thais to the west and the Annamites to the east. The Khmer empire would ultimately fall to the Thais. But the greatness that was Angkor had already passed, consumed by the unrelenting demands of serving the gods. And in time the capital would succumb to another invader, one that closed in from all sides: the relentless and advancing jungle.

Some 1,500 miles to the south of Angkor, on the Indonesian island of Java, stands the vast Buddhist monument of Borobudur. In size and shape alone, Borobudur is a remarkable structure: A temple mountain, 400 feet by 400 feet at its base, it rises from central Java's Kedu Plain in a series of six square and three circular terraces to a crowning bell-shaped stupa, the traditional moundlike burial edifice and religious symbol of Buddhism.

But ever since its discovery by Europeans in 1814, Borobudur had been recognized as an extraordinary monument—not only in its dimensions but in the complexity of its meaning. Around each of its levels is a walkway lined with some 1,460 carved stone panels and more than 500 statues of Buddha that teach the tenets of the faith. A huge pagoda perched atop the monument may represent the final entry into Nirvana. Borobudur was, in effect, a demonstration of the road to enlightenment, a Buddhist vision of the cosmos chiseled in stone.

Then, in 1885, the Dutch engineer J. W. IJzerman discovered on Borobudur's north side that one stone had fallen away from the wall that supported the walkway around the base. Inside he noticed a joint seam between the stones. The seam appeared to have

no purpose, unless the original design of the base had been different from its finished state. Intrigued, he removed about a yard of stones to reveal what had been the original wall. Not only did the discovery signify that the shape of the monument had been different; IJzerman also found that adorning the base was a complete series of reliefs. The carvings had been preserved in pristine condition *(pages 102-103)*.

IJzerman surmised that the addition of the second wall on top of the decorated base had become necessary during the building of Borobudur. Over one million blocks of stone had been used for the monument, which was, in effect, a stone sheath covering a natural hill. Architects must have added a reinforcing embankment around the original base—dubbed the "hidden foot"—to prevent the stonework from being pushed out by the weight above. Five years after IJzerman's find, a Dutch team removed the whole embankment in sections a few yards wide. Each section was carefully replaced before the next was removed to avoid the same danger of collapse that had caused the embankment to be built in the first place. During the operation, 160 reliefs were revealed in all.

Depicted on the reliefs of the hidden foot were scenes of worldly pleasure and the punishments of the world to come. Some had barely been finished before they were permanently hidden behind the support wall—and one even retained its chiseled workmens'

Trees sprout from the galleries and terraces of Borobudur as visitors stroll the grounds in this illustration based on drawings done in 1814 by H. C. Cornelius, the Dutch engineer who led the first effort to clear centuries of growth from the monument. The image, which appeared in 1830 in the second edition of Lieutenant Governor Thomas Stamford Raffles's book The History of Java, *is the first published view of the magnificent structure.*

100

inscriptions. From studying the style of the script—even allowing for the haste and carelessness with which the builders wrote—scholars have been able to estimate the approximate date of the monument. It had been built between AD 750 and 800, around the time of the great Khmer building period.

Since there are no certain contemporary references to the monument in inscriptions, this date provided a rare and vital clue to Borobudur's past. It placed Borobudur in the time of the mysterious Sailendras, the dynasty that ruled central Java from AD 778 to

864. Little is known of the Sailendras, or of the people they governed. They had probably arisen from within the agrarian, village-based culture of Java, which had inherited from India both the Hindu and Buddhist religions. Whatever their origins, their power must have been great, for it was the Sailendras who had eventually assumed the mantle from Funan of "Kings of the Mountain." It was against their influence that Jayavarman II had bridled when founding the Angkorian *mandala* in 802. And Sailendra domination of central Java had expelled to the east of the island a rival Hindu dynasty called Sanjaya.

But Borobudur has little to say about the people who built it. Modern archaeologists calculate from the amount of stone in the monument—which all came from a nearby riverbed—that its construction must have taken some 70 years, drawing on labor from among the farming communities of the Kedu Plain. Such a project must have had the support of the king. And yet Borobudur seems never to have been intended as a specifically royal monument like the temple mountains of Angkor. There is no room for royal rituals; there are no barriers or enclosing walls; nothing suggests it was a monument reserved for the elite. Although they remain virtually invisible, it seems that this was a place built for the people.

The focus of scholarly research at Borobudur has been fixed on the building's meaning. For the shape of the monument expresses the very beliefs that created it. To Buddhists, Borobudur was where the Holy met the Human. Over the centuries, visiting pilgrims have made their symbolic spiritual ascent of the monument, spiraling up from the everyday world to the state of Nirvana. This was done by passing clockwise around each of the terraces in succession, a walk of about three miles in all. Climbing the lower, square terraces—which depict events in the life of Buddha—the pilgrims passed from one realm of Buddhist theology to another, from the Sphere of Desires into the Sphere of Forms. On reaching Borobudur's three circular platforms—which carry no ornament at all—they entered the Sphere of Formlessness, the higher realm of detachment from the world. Here views across the landscape symbolized the pilgrims' widening spiritual horizons. The great stupa that crowns the monument serves as its 10th level. This number, archaeologists believe, is a reference to the 10 stages through which a Bodhisattva accumulates the virtue to become divine.

A century or so after Borobudur was built, however, the power of the Buddhist Sailendras was in decline. The rival Sanjaya dynasty—although displaced to eastern Java—remained powerful. Around AD 850, legends and inscriptions suggest, a Sailen-

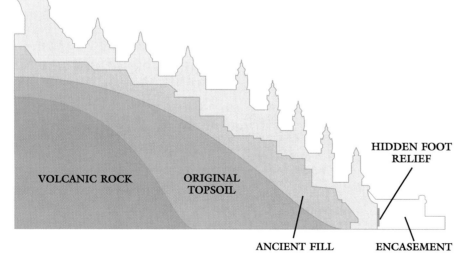

VOLCANIC ROCK

ORIGINAL TOPSOIL

ANCIENT FILL

HIDDEN FOOT RELIEF

ENCASEMENT

A cross section of Borobudur reveals the hill—and chunks of volcanic rock—around which the massive eighth-century Buddhist monument was built. The so-called hidden foot, a series of reliefs, can be seen in the lower right corner; the reliefs were covered over by a wall built soon after Borobudur's completion to keep the tiers from slipping. A chance discovery in 1885 brought them to light; after study, all but four were sealed away again. The one at right depicting vice and virtue contrasts the bawdy action of dancers and musicians with the modest demeanor of the respectable family to their right.

dra prince named Balaputra was driven by his ambition to become Java's supreme ruler—and into waging war against the Sanjaya king. The Sailendra lost and fled to the neighboring island of Sumatra, leaving the Sanjaya to dominate Java. No more great Buddhist monuments would be built on the island. But by 928 the Sanjaya civilization itself came to an end, eclipsed in what later inscriptions referred to only as a "calamity." With few clues to go on, archaeologists have proposed a range of explanations for what might have happened on the island: a volcanic eruption, disease, drought, or even a revenge attack by the Sailendras from Sumatra. Like the carved base of Borobudur—unseen for hundreds of years—the truth remains hidden.

As the mysterious builders of Borobudur were eclipsed in Java, a longer-lived culture was growing in another part of Southeast Asia. From its capital city nestled within a bend of the Irrawaddy River, the kingdom of Pagan in Burma would flourish until around the end of the 12th century. The monuments that still mark its site are noteworthy for their quality—and for their sheer number. Studded over a dusty plain of little more than 30 square miles are some 2,217 red-brick stupas, temples, and monasteries, glowing like jewels, with occasional white flamelike spires reaching into the sky—"an epic stage that has lost its cast," according to one visitor.

As at Angkor, the ruined city gave early Western visitors their first intimation of the past glories achieved by a people they had considered little more than primitive. During the early 19th century, European descriptions of Pagan had grown in frequency. After visiting

the site in 1827, Scots Orientalist John Crawfurd observed, "The vast extent of the ruins of Pagan, and the extent and splendor of its religious edifices, may be considered by some as proofs of considerable civilization among the Burmans." Twenty-eight years later the Scots soldier Henry Yule drew on his experience as a military engineer to make the first survey of some of Pagan's monuments. "The whole, as seen from the river," he wrote in 1855, "might pass for a scene in another planet, so fantastic and unearthly was the architecture."

Pagan is indeed a remarkable place. And yet its surviving monuments represent only a small portion of the 13,000 that once crowded the city and the surrounding plain. Despite limited access to the site, and scant resources for excavation, new discoveries constantly attest to the dedication of this society to serving its gods.

British rule in Burma began in 1886. But in archaeological terms, Pagan fared less well under the British than did the parts of Southeast Asia that came under French rule. During this period, research at Pagan continued as a largely piecemeal affair. The names of many of its lesser-known monuments were inaccurate, for example, made up by a local village headman to satisfy a visiting representative of the British Archaeological Survey of India. In 1912, however, a Cambridge graduate named Gordon Luce came to the Burmese capital, Rangoon, to teach in the Government College. His efforts would mark a decisive change. Luce became obsessed by the country, marrying a local woman and delving into Pagan's history. His life's work would confirm him as the preeminent expert in the field.

To aid his research, Luce trained one of his servants to make rubbings, then sent the man off to search for undiscovered inscriptions. For Luce believed that inscriptions held the key to understanding Pagan, and he set about learning the Old Burmese and Mon languages in which they were written. The ancient tongues posed few problems for the Englishman. In the words of one admirer, "Languages which other men require a lifetime to master became his linguistic tool within a few years." His pioneering research laid a foundation for the study of Pagan's inscriptions.

Once again, the world revealed by the epigraphs was one in which elaborate building projects were motivated by the desire to earn religious merit. And in the case of Pagan, the religion was Theravada Buddhism, an ascetic, scripture-based form of the faith. Such merit could be earned by all of the city's inhabitants—be they slaves or kings—by good works, such as the building and maintenance of

An approaching storm darkens the sky as sunlight illuminates temples, monasteries, and stupas dotting the Burmese plain of Pagan, site of a vanished city. During Pagan's heyday, from the mid-11th century AD to 1287, it was densely packed with structures built of teak and other perishable materials. Only the religious monuments, constructed of durable fired brick, remain standing.

temples. Once earned, merit could also be shared. In one dedicatory inscription the foster mother of a Pagan king expressed her wish that the salvation she might earn would spread to the peoples across the "countless world systems." Another inscription records how one merit earner donated cows, land, and laborers to a monastery in the expectation that the "benefit of this offering I have given—the present king, future kings, [my] mother and father, [my] sons and all creatures, may they benefit equally with me."

Theravada Buddhism became Pagan's dominant religion in AD 1056, taking precedence over the religion's earlier forms and the folk worship of nature spirits. The change had come by order of Anawrahta, traditionally regarded as the founder of the Pagan kingdom. But excavation of the city's brick fortification wall showed that there had been an urban center at Pagan 200 years before Anawrahta.

Sometime during the ninth century, Luce believed, the ancestors of today's Burmese had left their homeland on the Chinese-Tibetan border to settle in central Burma among the Pyu people already living there. As the newcomers achieved gradual dominance, they learned from the Pyu wet-rice agriculture, providing the foundation of the early city-states from which Pagan would emerge. The Buddhist Pyu built the first stupa at Pagan during the ninth or 10th centuries. But the city's real growth only began when Anawrahta succeeded to the throne in AD 1044.

The new king built up Pagan's defenses and created new irrigation works. For these projects he needed additional money and manpower, however, and in 1057 his army moved downriver to sack Thaton, the capital of the Irrawaddy Delta kingdom of Mon. "The great capital of Thaton was in ruin," lamented a Mon chronicler, "and silence reigned supreme. In contrast, Pagan shone in glory and in triumph, as if it had become the abode of gods."

Anawrahta channeled much of the wealth from the Thaton campaign into the hands of Buddhist leaders. He also brought some 30,000 Mon prisoners back to Pagan, including architects, craftsmen, and Theravada Buddhist monks, who would provide the impetus behind two centuries of remarkable religious construction: The builders of Pagan would average around two new pagodas every month. Such royal patronage of Buddhism at first stimulated Pagan's economic development. In time, it would threaten its very existence.

Near the eastern gate of the ancient city of Pagan, archaeologists discovered around 1990 what they thought was the site of the royal palace. Although the original structure had been built of wood—as at Angkor, stone was reserved for religious building—its brick substructure remained. The excavators uncovered a series of open-brick cylinders, about four feet in diameter and the same in height, that may have served as footholds for the great wooden pillars that once supported the building. The archaeologists' conclusions were backed up by a remarkable find. Examining an old manuscript, the Burmese epigrapher and historian U Maung Maung Tin came across a map that gave the precise measurements of the palace and its location in relation to the city gates. It confirmed that the substructure did indeed mark the site of the palace.

From here, Burmese monarchs ruled over a kingdom of remarkable diversity. "It was an age characterized by Burman military rule, Pyu traditions, Mon culture, and Theravadin culture." So wrote one historian of the reign of King Kyanzittha, which lasted from AD 1084 to 1111. Such a range of influences produced a real ferment of creation. Twenty-one years into Kyanzittha's reign, Pagan's architects and sculptors completed one of its outstanding monuments: the Ananda Temple *(page 112)*.

According to Burmese sources, the temple was inspired by the visit to the king's palace of eight Indian monks, begging for alms.

"You cannot move a hand or foot at Pagan without touching a sacred thing" goes a Burmese sentiment, given vivid expression in the photograph below showing a worker clearing dirt from the head of a Buddha discovered during 1992 excavations. More than 13,000 brick monuments once stood in the city, and even though thousands have been identified and excavated, thousands more wait underground for archaeologists to uncover them.

They told the king of their life in the legendary cave temples of the Himalaya Mountains, creating before him—through their powers of meditation—the snow-covered landscape. So enthralled was Kyanzittha with what he saw that he commissioned a replica temple in the plains of Pagan. When the structure was completed, the account continues, the king personally executed the unfortunate architect. Awed by what had been built, Kyanzittha was determined that the Ananda would never be duplicated.

The inside of the temple is gloomy. Its four teak Buddhas—

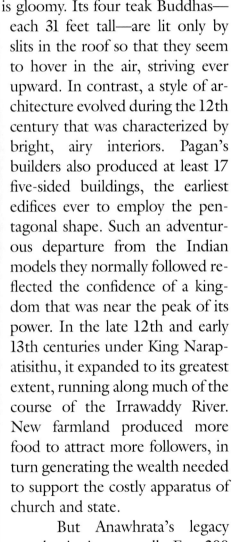

each 31 feet tall—are lit only by slits in the roof so that they seem to hover in the air, striving ever upward. In contrast, a style of architecture evolved during the 12th century that was characterized by bright, airy interiors. Pagan's builders also produced at least 17 five-sided buildings, the earliest edifices ever to employ the pentagonal shape. Such an adventurous departure from the Indian models they normally followed reflected the confidence of a kingdom that was near the peak of its power. In the late 12th and early 13th centuries under King Narapatisithu, it expanded to its greatest extent, running along much of the course of the Irrawaddy River. New farmland produced more food to attract more followers, in turn generating the wealth needed to support the costly apparatus of church and state.

But Anawhrata's legacy was beginning to tell. For 200 years, Buddhism had received large endowments from disciples eager to attain the merit path to salvation. This placed a considerable part of Pagan's riches beyond the reach of the state: While religious centers prospered, the revenues on which royal power depended were seriously drained. As one scholar observes, "The Kingdom of Pagan declined because the factors that had nurtured it in the first place became, in time, forces that contradicted and destroyed it." Like Angkor, a civilization that had grown up and thrived in the service of the gods would collapse under the burdens of that service.

In 1283, Kublai Khan took advantage of the kingdom's weakness and invaded. According to the Italian explorer Marco Polo—who had heard reports about Pagan but probably never visited—only clowns and jugglers were needed to conquer the land; Burmese accounts claim that the Mongol force amounted to six million mounted warriors and 20 million foot soldiers. The truth lies somewhere in between. As a cultural and religious center, Pagan would endure. But its golden age was over.

Mongol rule had little visible effect on Pagan. Natural forces have been less sparing, however. The Irrawaddy, for example, has washed away about one-third of the old city, and a 1975 earthquake damaged many of the remaining monuments. But archaeological treasures still turn up at Pagan—such as a votive tablet unearthed at the start of the 1990s by workers digging a hotel swimming pool. In recent times, the focus of research has moved away from the 19th-century concentration on inscriptions. Archaeologists have turned to the architecture and artifacts that Buddhism inspired. But as elsewhere in Southeast Asia, they face uncommon difficulties. The Burmese government keeps many away from Pagan; at Angkor, the unpredictable Khmer Rouge controls some of the territory on which the civilization's monuments stand. The legacy of the classical kingdoms that endured for centuries remains at the mercy of the unstable political situation of the contemporary world.

DAWNING OF A NEW BEAUTY

However uniquely Southeast Asian the art and architecture of Vietnam, Burma, Cambodia, Thailand, and Indonesia may seem, they have roots in India. The particular genius of the Southeast Asians was to absorb the Hindu and Buddhist religions brought by Indian teachers and traders as early as the first millennium AD—along with Hindu and Buddhist culture and art—and use them to their own ends. In the process, architects and artists—who were already skilled in the production of fine bronze and terra-cotta objects—developed styles and forms of expression that reflected regional tastes. Thus the temple scene above can be identified at a glance as Thai, because among other things, the statue of the seated Buddha sports a tall flame on top of his head (indicative of his inner spiritual heat) that is typically Thai in style. The flame's shape is echoed in the stupa on the far right.

The Southeast Asians incorporated many of the Buddhist and Hindu gods into their own pantheons. Southeast Asian rulers, in turn, used both Hinduism and Buddhism to increase their own spiritual prowess— a way of attracting followers and thus of increasing their temporal power. Growing wealth based on agricultural pursuits, such as rice cultivation and overland, river, and sea trade, provided the means with which they could construct multitiered temples and decorate them with images of Buddha, Shiva, and Vishnu based on Indian models.

This picture essay shows how the fusion of foreign ideas and local traditions helped lead to the rich artistic expression—and the stylistic diversity—for which Southeast Asia would be famous, a legacy that survives today in the area's numerous abandoned cities and magnificent temples.

VIETNAM: A BLENDING OF STYLES

Champa, the kingdom of the Chams, occupied various sites in southern Vietnam for more than 1,000 years, leaving behind many Hindu and Buddhist temples and stone sculptures. The Chams were in constant conflict with the Khmers to the west and the Vietnamese to the north; their power was finally usurped in the 15th century AD by the Vietnamese. One of the last Cham temples built is seen below, at a place called Po Klaung Garai. It was dedicated to the Hindu god Shiva, who is depicted inside as a stylized phallus, or linga, with a face thought to be that of the king and outside, over the carved east entrance, as a dancer.

This seventh-century-AD sandstone Vishnu, probably from Vietnam's Mekong Delta, home of the Cham people, was once supported by a stone arch, a bit of which clings to the crown. The use of an arch and the simple, yet powerful modeling of the figure are hallmarks of early Cham art.

An 11th-century makara, *a fantastic water beast* (below), *disgorges a sword-wielding warrior. Other* makaras *can be seen just below the corner roof towers of the temple at far left. Of Indian derivation, the* makara *was to become associated in art with the Chinese and Vietnamese dragon.*

The Hindu god Shiva and his consort Parvati (above), *shown with the bull that traditionally served as his royal mount, decorate a 24-inch-tall 11th-century sandstone linga. Shiva's imposing headdress is adorned with curling designs, a common motif in Cham art.*

Sited on the Irrawady River in central Burma, the city of Pagan lay at a cultural crossroads used by traders, diplomats, and Buddhist monks from India, China, and Southeast Asia. Founded in the ninth century AD, Pagan was the first Burmese kingdom. There had been earlier kingdoms composed of two groups, the Mon and Pyu, whose art and culture were already Indianized and on whose achievements the Burmese relied in turning Pagan into a city of 13,000 Buddhist temples and stupas.

The flowering of Burmese art and architecture began in the reign of Anawrahta (1044-1077). Adhering to Theravada Buddhism, in which the laity's sup-

port of monks enabled the givers to accrue merit for future lives, Anawrahta launched a building campaign. A later king, Kyanzittha (1084-1113), constructed the Ananda temple, above, which was inspired by Indian models but also incorporates Mon and Pyu elements, such as the crosslike ground plan. The Pagan temples were decorated inside with brightly colored murals that illustrated the life of Buddha and depicted aspects of court life and outside with stucco carvings of animals and floral patterns, all executed in a unique Burmese style.

A painted scene from the life of Buddha covers a detail of this fragile, 12th-century-AD piece of cloth, discovered in 1984 in Pagan rolled up and folded inside a lacquered wood statue of Buddha. Artists painted similar scenes on the interior walls of many of Pagan's temples.

A gold-repoussé and black-lacquer plaque (left) from the eighth century AD, showing a seated Buddha with elongated earlobes and a serene smile, was crafted by a skilled Pyu artisan.

Carved from a tree trunk around the 12th century AD, the six-foot-tall statue at right still bears traces of gold leaf and black and red lacquer. Scholars debate the figure's identity; it may be a portrait of a dead Pagan royal personage, idealized as a Bodhi-sattva or perhaps a crowned Buddha.

113

INDONESIA: AN ISLAND CHANGE

The Indonesian islands of Java, Bali, and Sumatra attracted Indian traders seeking spices, gold, and silver, among other things. The Indonesians, whose traditions were steeped in ancestor worship and animistic cults, responded to the supernatural aspects of Hinduism—numerous gods, mythical creatures, nature spirits—and to the rites associated with Tantric Buddhism.

Using these aspects of Indian religions the Indonesians created monuments, building some with bathing pools that combined Indian notions of water's ritual cleansing power and indigenous ideas of its fructifying nature. Above, water nymphs serve as spouts at a 1,000-year-old bathing pool in Bali, where a peculiarly Indonesian form of Hinduism is practiced today.

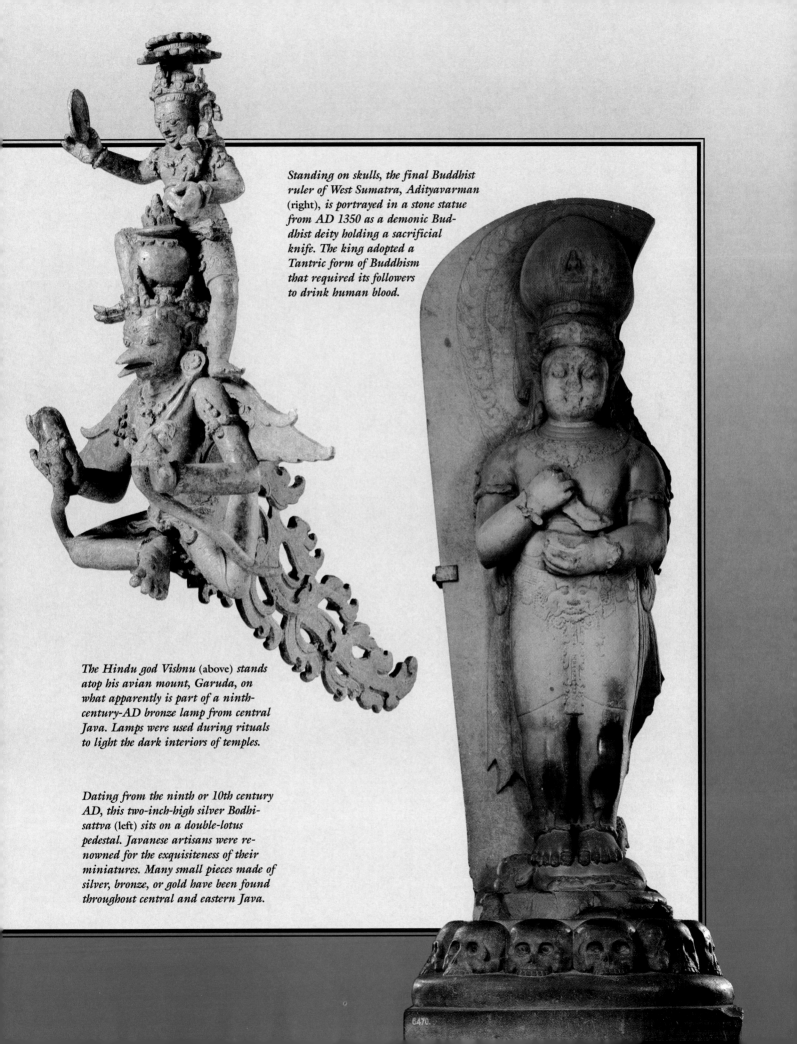

Standing on skulls, the final Buddhist ruler of West Sumatra, Adityavarman *(right), is portrayed in a stone statue from AD 1350 as a demonic Buddhist deity holding a sacrificial knife. The king adopted a Tantric form of Buddhism that required its followers to drink human blood.*

The Hindu god Vishnu *(above) stands atop his avian mount, Garuda, on what apparently is part of a ninth-century-AD bronze lamp from central Java. Lamps were used during rituals to light the dark interiors of temples.*

Dating from the ninth or 10th century AD, this two-inch-high silver Bodhisattva *(left) sits on a double-lotus pedestal. Javanese artisans were renowned for the exquisiteness of their miniatures. Many small pieces made of silver, bronze, or gold have been found throughout central and eastern Java.*

CAMBODIA: HEAVEN ON EARTH

In central Cambodia, seat of the powerful Khmer empire, local talent and traditions merged with concepts of Indian Buddhist and Hindu beliefs to produce art such as the world had not seen before. Stone carvers of the pre-Angkor era had already mastered sculpture in the round—as seen in this seventh-century-AD Ganesha, the Hindu god of fortune *(right)*—at a time when their Indian counterparts were still working primarily in relief. The bare torso, lack of ornamentation, and scant, lightly incised clothing of the figure reflect a Cambodian taste that later would translate into the commanding images of the Angkorian kingdom.

After Jayavarman II founded Angkor in AD 802, the Khmer applied themselves over the next four centuries to the construction of multitiered stone temples dedicated to Hindu and Buddhist gods and to their kings, whom they regarded as earthly forms of the deities themselves. In doing so, Khmer artists and architects believed that they were creating heaven on earth.

In this detail from a 160-foot-long, 12th-century-AD relief at Angkor Wat, the demon Ravana and his army pull the multiheaded Naga to churn the cosmic ocean, while delicate Apsaras—celestial nymphs—flutter overhead. The relief illustrates an episode from the Hindu creation epic known as the Churning of the Sea of Milk, a favorite of the Khmers.

The massive face of the king as the compassionate Bodhisattva Avalokitesvara tops a stone tower at the Bayon temple complex at Angkor. Built during the reign of the great Buddhist Khmer ruler Jayavarman VII, the temple, with 200 giant faces installed on its 50 towers, has mystified and astounded vistors for centuries.

Wearing a crown and jewelry of a type frequently seen on Khmer-period images from Angkor Wat, this 12th-century-AD, 14-inch-tall bronze and gilt figure may represent the Hindu goddess Uma or may possibly be a portrait of a royal lady who identified herself with the goddess.

THAILAND: ART CLOSE TO THE SOURCE

Thai coastal towns were significant ports for Indian and Chinese merchants, and some of the oldest Southeast Asian art to display Hindu and Buddhist influence comes from them. In central Thailand an early Buddhist culture associated with the people known as the Mon created thousands of artifacts, including the seventh-century-AD Wheel of the Law shown on the opposite page.

When the Thais first entered the historical record, around the 12th century AD, they were under the Angkorian Khmer, but in time managed to found their own capital at Sukhothai in the north. The sleek and elegant art style of the Sukhothai period has become an emblem of Thailand, one of the world's surviving strongholds of Buddhism. In the 11th century the Angkorian Khmer began ruling parts of the country, and many Khmer-style temples were constructed, including the one above, its balustrades adorned with Nagas.

Borrowing iconography from India, artisans of the seventh or eighth century AD in what is today Thailand sculpted this three-foot-tall limestone wheel to express the Buddhist doctrine Dharma-cakra, Wheel of the Law. The deer alludes to Deer Park in India, where Buddha preached his first sermon.

A masterpiece of Sukhothai bronze casting, this 14th-century figure is known as the Walking Buddha. Sukhothai artists were the first to create an image in the round of the Buddha in motion, his right foot lifted from the ground and his left hand raised in the gesture known as Dispelling Fear.

Excavated from a site at Nakon Pathom, Thailand, the 11-inch-tall stucco head of Buddha at left, modeled in the eighth century AD, exhibits the facial features of the Mon people who occupied the region during that period.

LESSONS IN CONSERVATION LEARNED THE HARD WAY

The serene visage of a king in the guise of Buddha peers through vegetation at Ta Som in Angkor. The roots of a strangler fig embrace the head, while the tree's greenery forms a leafy crown.

In the summer of 1969, the Vietnam War was raging fiercely around the area of Mi Son, site of a magnificent temple complex built by the Cham, a people who had dominated the coastal plains of Vietnam for almost a millennium—from the fourth to the 13th centuries AD. Located about 43 miles southwest of the city of Danang in central Vietnam, the complex had been richly endowed with temples by successive generations of rulers. The earliest, wooden structures have left little trace, but from the seventh century onward, brick-and-sandstone edifices steadily took their place. By the 12th century, when construction came to a halt, about 70 religious monuments crowded the valley, forming a sacred precinct of unique size and importance. Twenty or so still remain.

The centerpiece of the complex, the 70-foot-high Mi Son Tower, was being used in that war-racked summer as a hideout and an arms dump by the Vietcong, who had also mounted a radio transmitter on its summit. And then on August 8, after air force bombing runs had failed to knock out the tower, a U.S. commando team crept in and planted explosives. The blast reduced to a pile of rubble a magnificent structure that had been called the masterpiece of the Cham.

The fate of the Mi Son Tower is a vivid illustration of the dangers confronting much of Southeast Asia's architectural heritage in the troubled 20th century. The shadow of conflict has rarely been far

121

away. The region had hardly emerged from World War II when it was embroiled in a succession of anticolonial struggles and independence wars, which in turn paved the way for the Communist insurgences of the 1960s and 1970s. The violence rose to a crescendo of senseless slaughter in Cambodia during the Khmer Rouge ascendancy from 1975 to 1979. Only in the 1980s did something approaching peace descend on the region; and even today political divisions still create impediments to full-scale conservation.

Yet such work is vital in a region where tropical vegetation is always waiting to stifle and to smother the works of man. For centuries Borobudur and most of the temples of Angkor were overwhelmed by nature, swallowed up by the encroaching forest like Sleeping Beauty's castle in the fairy tale. Without constant surveillance, they could quickly revert to a similar state.

But nature can be a preserver as well as a destructive force. Sandstone or volcanic-andesite reliefs protected under a layer of humus are less likely to suffer degradation than are those exposed to the erosive effects of the monsoon rains. Paradoxically, the monuments unearthed by 19th-century explorers and archaeologists are often at more risk when poorly maintained than those left in their original condition.

Other natural phenomena can be more abrupt in their effects than creeping vegetation. Much of the region is in an earthquake zone. The extent of the threat became apparent in 1975, when the imperial city of Pagan in Burma was shaken by a tremor that destroyed entire temples. Seismographic evidence indicates that the possibility of a second, similar disaster cannot be ruled out.

Yet nature has not been responsible for the worst of the

In 1900 the French architect, artist, and archaeologist Henri Parmentier went to Vietnam to study Cham architecture. His drawing at left illustrates a masterpiece of Cham construction—the lavishly ornamented tower at Mi Son—that was destroyed by U.S. forces in 1969, leaving only rubble behind (above). Parmentier, who spent the rest of his life in Southeast Asia, founded an archaeological center in Mi Son and published a comprehensive study of Cham art and architecture before his death in Phnom Penh in 1949.

damage done to Southeast Asia's monuments in recent decades. Human depredation—in particular the looting of sculptures and bas-reliefs—has been a problem at almost all the major sites. The growing market for Southeast Asian antiquities has been fed by a stream of objects hacked, sawed, and stolen from their original locations. Governmental regulations aimed at stopping the plunder have proved difficult to enforce under the best of conditions and virtually inoperative in time of war. The cumulative effect on the region's heritage has been devastating.

To be sure, Southeast Asia is not alone in the world when it comes to the plundering of archaeological sites. In Latin America, for example, there is a brisk trade in pilfered Inca and Maya artifacts, and some experts estimate that, even today, huge numbers of ancient Egyptian artifacts are being taken from the necropolis at Saqqara, site of the first pyramid.

Among the various dangers on the depressing list of factors assailing the sites of Southeast Asia—warfare, earthquake, the ravages of nature, looting—warfare has probably done the least direct damage. In this respect the sad case of the Mi Son Tower is exceptional,

123

The roots of a silk-cotton tree appear to melt into the stones and down the sides of a stone wall at Angkor. The seeds of these trees, and the equally destructive strangler fig, are deposited in the ruins by birds and germinate quickly. The trees grow more than 100 feet high, their woody roots penetrating between the stones and dislodging them. When the tree dies the weakened structures collapse.

and the example of Borobudur more typical. During the Java War, a 19th-century native uprising against Dutch colonial rule, fighting took place close to the temple, but neither side put it to military use and it survived intact.

In recent times the greatest threat has been to Angkor, which for much of the 1970s and 1980s was embroiled in the internecine rivalries of the Cambodian civil war. For a decade after 1972 the area around the temple was off-limits to Westerners, and dire rumors spread about the devastation it had suffered during the fighting.

So observers were happily surprised, when access to the district was finally restored, to find that for the most part the combatants had respected the monuments. An American journalist who vis-

A SORRY STORY OF PLUNDER AND GREED

In the late 1890s, after years of war and civil unrest, Burmese companies specializing in cargo and mail service began offering European tourists accommodations on steamers bound for the ancient city of Pagan. One traveler making the journey was Theodor Thomann, a German who—along with five companions—arrived in Pagan in June 1899. After setting up residence in a monastery on the banks of the Irrawaddy River, the visitors began to plunder the treasures of the ancient temples.

A letter of introduction from the German emperor allowed Thomann access to ancient sites, and within three months he had ruthlessly removed hundreds of wall paintings from the buildings. By the time the authorities became aware of the theft it was too late; the treasures had been sent to Germany. Expelled from Burma, Thomann went home and, after months of negotiations, sold the artifacts to a Hamburg museum, turning a tidy profit for himself.

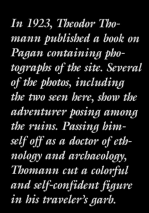

In 1923, Theodor Thomann published a book on Pagan containing photographs of the site. Several of the photos, including the two seen here, show the adventurer posing among the ruins. Passing himself off as a doctor of ethnology and archaeology, Thomann cut a colorful and self-confident figure in his traveler's garb.

ited Angkor in 1982 noted occasional bullet holes on carvings and statuary, and shrapnel had pockmarked one of Angkor Wat's celebrated bas-reliefs. Given the massive size of the complex, however, the damage was slight, and he was able to summarize his survey of the buildings by reporting that "amazingly, they are nearly unscathed by the years of war."

Despite the relative lack of physical degradation, the impact of the breakdown of government was nonetheless immense. Before the war the Angkor Conservancy, which had responsibility for the upkeep of the monument, was an unusually well-provided body. It owned 100 vehicles including a 200-foot crane, and also had its own air-conditioned laboratories, power plants, and weather stations. In-

A mural the Germans left behind bears the scars of the thieves' attempts to carve it off the wall. Saws—which were used to remove the paintings —caused irreparable damage to the priceless works.

come to support its work came from the Cambodian government, Prince Sihanouk, France, and from the 70,000 tourists who visited the monuments each year. Two luxury hotels had recently been completed with a view to boosting the numbers.

The upsurge of hostilities quickly changed all that. Bernard-Philippe Groslier, the French scholar in charge of conservation, was forced out in 1972. By 1981, when the first attempts to resume his work began, tourist traffic had dwindled to a trickle, and the technical resources available to the conservancy's new, Cambodian director had been reduced to a single truck and a bicycle.

A member of Rome's International Center for the Study of Preservation and Conservation of Cultural Property cleans a textile fragment, part of a 12th-century painting found in a Buddhist temple in Pagan after the 1975 earthquake. Extremely fragile, the cloth artwork disintegrated soon after it was discovered. Resembling the pieces of a jigsaw puzzle, the fragments were sent to Rome, where the conservators—headed by the husband-and-wife team of Carlo Giantomassi and Zari Donatella—spent more than a year painstakingly restoring the painting.

More lamentable, most of the Cambodians whom Groslier had been training to carry on his work had been killed. The Khmer Rouge—the Communist insurgents who marched triumphantly into Phnom Penh in 1975—imposed a reign of terror during their four years in power. They dreamed of creating a nation of self-sustaining cultivators who would relive the glory days of the original Angkor empire. In pursuit of this vision, the towns were emptied, and the middle classes were forced, in the name of political reeducation, to work the land under the suspicious eyes of peasant commissars who were encouraged to deal with any sign of dissent by killing the offenders. In practice, any mark of special education or culture—knowledge of a foreign language, even past contact with foreigners—could be enough to condemn someone to sudden death in the nation's killing fields. By a bitter irony, the guerrillas who dreamed of returning to the agriculturally based paradise they believed the Angkor civilization to have been effectively wiped out a generation of the very Cambodians who could have helped preserve that civilization's surviving monuments.

As a result, the war's legacy was an Angkor invaded once more by nature and showing dangerous symptoms of structural neglect. There were also more sinister mementos of the fighting. Minefields are to this day a continuing problem in the locality, and fatalities are common when people step on an unseen mine. One of the priority tasks confronting those currently responsible for the monuments has been to identify the danger areas and establish clearly marked restricted areas so as to prevent further deaths. Guerrilla activity has also been slow to recede. As recently as 1995, Khmer Rouge fighters operating from the jungle to the north of Angkor were able to take temporary control of the 10th-century Banteay Srei, threatening to destroy the monument if they were attacked while in possession of it.

While the damage Angkor suffered in the civil war stretched over two decades, the devastation of the magnificent ruins at Pagan occurred within minutes. The earthquake that rocked the site on July 8, 1975, has been called "perhaps the worst natural disaster to take place in an archaeological district in modern times." Brickwork cracked and crumbled, some smaller edifices were entirely consumed, and many irreplaceable mural paintings were destroyed.

But in a curious irony, the earthquake revealed some previously unknown treasures. It was usual for Pagan's builders to seal small relics inside the statues of the Buddha that graced the temples. The force of the quake split several of these open, disgorging their contents for the first time in 900 years. A painting on cotton depicting scenes from the life of the Buddha was uncovered in this way; it had been rolled around a bamboo stick and placed in a cavity in a statue's arm. Another, similar image came to light in the wreckage of a relic chamber in the building's upper section. Most remarkable of these discoveries was a series of small reliefs of seated Buddhas surrounded by scenes

Its colors still remarkably fresh after almost 1,000 years, this portion of the 32- by 55-inch painting depicting scenes from the life of Buddha illustrates the skill of the painter and the conservators. According to the restorers "the painting is clearly still quite delicate and thus should not be exposed to excessive fluctuations in temperature and humidity." In addition, it must be protected from direct sunlight, dust, and pollutants.

depicting incidents from the religious leader's life. The finest measures just 5 by 2½ inches, yet contains no fewer than 78 separate figures. Unfortunately, most of the remaining statues have now been shattered by people hoping to find similar treasures.

Wars and natural disasters have affected individual sites, but the problem of plundering has been endemic to almost all of them. Even Pagan has suffered, despite the restrictions on freedom of movement imposed by the successive governments that have ruled Burma since the country gained independence from Britain in 1948. Objects are nonetheless rumored to be smuggled out of the country by foreign embassy officials in diplomatic baggage.

Borobudur lost many artworks in the century after its rediscovery in 1814. The objects from its holy of holies, the shrine at the topmost pinnacle of the monument, are said to have been removed sometime shortly after that date and are now lost. It has been suggested that the entire monument may have been built as a vast reliquary designed to hold a portion of the remains of the Buddha that were released by the third-century-BC Indian ruler Asoka from their original depositories so they could be shared with the world. All that is now known of the shrine's contents, however, is a report that they consisted of a small quantity of ashy material enclosed in a lidded metal urn, along with a metal image and a few coins.

Thieves got to the Mendut—a Buddhist shrine of similar date that stands two miles from Borobudur—earlier still, raiding it even before clearing operations were undertaken in 1836. The workmen who unearthed it from beneath a canopy of volcanic sand and tropical vegetation found that its walls had been pierced and treasure hunters had either carried off or smashed all the smaller freestanding statuary it contained.

At Borobudur itself the problem of pilfering grew from about the mid-19th century onward as the number of visitors increased. Sometime before 1850, a hut with a stone seat was constructed at the highest point of the sanctuary to allow tourists to admire the view in comfort *(page 101)*. Some insisted on taking small carvings and statuary as souvenirs of their trip. The situation was compounded by local villagers, who started removing stones from the ancient monuments as a convenient construction material. In the 1880s sections of the Mendut were used to build a bridge.

WAR AND PEACE IN ANGKOR

Pich Keo, the Cambodian seen in the photograph at right, is a survivor. For years he worked with Bernard-Philippe Groslier, curator of the École Française d'Extrême Orient (EFEO), to conserve and restore the temples of Angkor. In the early 1970s war forced the French out of Angkor leaving the young man to fend for himself. Pich Keo was lucky; during the dark years of Khmer Rouge control millions of people, and almost all of the educated class, were killed. The few who survived were sent to work the rice fields for the new regime.

In 1979 the Khmer Rouge was pushed out of Angkor by the Vietnamese, and Pich Keo, with several hundred other Cambodians who had worked at the site before the bloodbath, returned to find the temples overgrown with vegetation, littered with trash, and covered with messages left by people hoping to find lost relatives. Rumors of battles fought inside the complex proved false and the temples had not been destroyed, as Pich Keo had feared. Though the years of neglect had a serious effect on the buildings, damage attributable to fighting was relatively slight.

Shortly after his return to Angkor, Pich Keo was appointed chairman of the Committee to Conserve Angkor and he and his small band of workers, with

Pich Keo examines a statue of Buddha at Angkor, painted with ritual tattoos by believers in hopes the markings will bring protection.

few supplies and almost no equipment, began the task of maintaining and caring for the complex under the close eye of Vietnamese soldiers. It would be years before agreements could be worked out between Cambodia and UNESCO so that, with financial aid and expertise from the international community, the real work of conservation and restoration could begin. For now, a handful of Cambodians headed by a determined young man would take on the job of saving one of the great treasures of the world.

At this unhappy period, conservation of the monument was in the hands of the manager of a local government-run guesthouse, and supervision was grossly inadequate. Soldiers stationed in the vicinity are said to have made use of Borobudur's stone Buddha images to sharpen their swords, while officers finished dinner parties by staging mock assaults on the shrine.

Worse was to come, in the form of an extraordinary act of diplomatic vandalism carried out with the knowledge and approval of the Dutch authorities. In 1896 the king of Siam paid an official visit to Borobudur. His hosts marked the occasion by letting the visiting monarch help himself to any artworks that were not structurally attached to the monument. The king—a connoisseur of Asian art—responded by taking back to Bangkok eight cartloads of statues and reliefs, many of them of the highest quality. Small wonder that one foreign observer, writing shortly after the turn of the century, should claim that "the neglect of the ancient monuments of Java has been nothing short of scandalous."

In fact, the situation was by that time already starting to improve. In 1900 the site was finally protected by a substantial fence, and extra caretakers were hired to guard it. A commission was set up to study the condition of the monument, and its report—published in 1902—marked the start of serious attempts at conservation. Today, Borobudur is one of the best protected (and one of the most visited) of the region's archaeological attractions, and in many ways stands as a model for other authorities to follow.

The lessons of Borobudur badly need to be learned at Ban Chiang in Thailand, which has in recent decades been more thoroughly despoiled by looters than any other site of comparable importance in Southeast Asia. The discovery by Stephen Young of a trove of pottery dating back 2,000 to 5,000 years set in motion a rush for profit that almost succeeded in destroying the mound's value for serious archaeological investigation.

Increased official attention together with a diminishing supply of finds finally succeeded in reducing unauthorized excavation at Ban Chiang itself by the end of the 1970s. Sadly, however, the looting did not stop; the treasure hunters simply turned their attention to other mounds in the region. Archaeologist Chester Gorman, who played a leading role in excavating Southeast Asian sites, was horri-

Thieves squat among stolen statues at the police station at Siem Reap on the outskirts of Angkor. Years of war and political instability led to weak legal protection, ineffective law enforcement, and lax security measures, allowing cultural objects to cross the 500-mile unprotected border between Cambodia and Thailand. Local peasants are paid as little as $10 for each sculpture, which then may be sold for many times that on the black market.

fied by the damage being done. Shortly before his death in 1981, he publicized his concerns in an article for the journal *Art Research News*. In the article he described how some Thai and foreign society figures had "used their status and fortunes to destroy totally some of the most important sites on the Khorat Plateau." Gorman concluded bleakly that "in the last five years of survey, no unlooted site has been located."

If Ban Chiang had borne the brunt of the plundering in the 1970s, the black marketeers turned their attention in the following decade increasingly to Angkor. The complex already had a long history of rapine. The most famous culprit was the French writer André Malraux—a future minister of culture under the presidency of World War II hero General Charles de Gaulle—who in 1923, as a young man of 21, set out with his bride from Paris with the express intention of stealing a relief from the recently discovered site of Banteay Srei. He was arrested with the piece in Phnom Penh and condemned to three years' imprisonment, reduced to a one-year suspended sentence on appeal. In fact he never went to prison.

Theft continued to be enough of a problem in the ensuing decades for the complex's French guardians to take preventive measures. Some important objects were sent to Phnom Penh to join the collections of the country's national museum. Other pieces of merit were kept on site in the guarded storeroom of the Angkor Conservancy.

Ironically enough, looting ceased almost entirely in the late 1970s—the years of the Khmer Rouge ascendancy. Fierce Cambodian nationalists, the regime's leaders looked back on the Angkor period as a golden age, and they protected its monuments accordingly. Under their savage rule, fear proved an effective deterrent to looting.

The situation changed in 1979, when Vietnamese troops invaded the country, and the Viet-backed government of Heng Samrinh was installed in Phnom Penh. The remaining Khmer Rouge

forces took to the jungle to conduct a guerrilla campaign, and the area around Angkor became a war zone.

Government control of the district remained insecure well into the 1990s, and the unsettled conditions proved highly propitious for art thieves. It was rumored that the Khmer Rouge themselves, forsaking their former principles, had taken to looting statuary and selling it across the border into Thailand in return for hard currency with which to continue their struggle. Thai military officers with contacts on the Bangkok art market were said to be actively and lucratively involved in the trade. Other individuals no doubt took advantage of the general confusion to traffic to their own advantage.

Although the situation was a murky one, what was certain was that some highly organized thieving was going on, and that it included for the first time direct assaults by armed bands on the storerooms of the Angkor Conservancy itself. In 1993 a commando group equipped with hand grenades and a rocket launcher broke down the wall of the compound and made off with 10 valuable stone sculptures. In another attack two months later, nine of the conservancy's guards were kidnapped at gunpoint and forced to carry sculpted Buddha heads into the surrounding countryside, before being released to return empty-handed.

Set up in the early 1900s and enlarged and improved in 1966 to accommodate laboratories and restoration workshops, the EFEO's Angkor Conservancy warehouses were filled with Khmer masterpieces when the French team, headed by Bernard-Philippe Groslier, had to evacuate in 1972. Once containing over 4,000 pieces, the warehouses, maintained by the Cambodians, now hold only 2,400 sculptures.

This gallery of sculpture stolen since 1970 from the warehouses at Angkor was featured in the spring 1994 issue of Minerva, *a periodical dedicated to ancient art. Editor-in-chief Jerome Eisenberg hopes "this publicity will result not only in the location and return of some of the pieces but will also send a signal to those who are encouraging the looting of cultural objects that such trafficking will not be tolerated by either museum professionals or those who collect and deal in Asian art."*

Stolen Objects

DCA 3874. Sandstone head of a deity with crown-like diadem. 13th century AD. 22 cm. From Banteay Samray temple, Angkor. Stolen in 1993 from the Dépôt.

DCA 4872. Sandstone head of Buddha, with traces of recent gilding. Late 12th-early 13th century AD. 28 cm. From Prab Khan temple, Kompong Svay. Stolen in 1993 from the Dépôt.

DC4611. Light grey sandstone body of the 4-armed Vishnu on a square pedestal. Mid-10th century AD. 84 cm. From Prasat Kravanh, Angkor. Stolen in 1993 from the Dépôt.

DCA4816. Sandstone torso of a 4-armed male figure. Second half of the 11th century AD. 89 cm. From the Prasat Ta Dong Temple, Angkor region. Stolen in 1993 from the Dépôt.

DCA 7081. Unfinished grey sandstone female torso. Late 10th century AD. 56 cm. From Pasat Trapeang Khna, Angkor region.

DCA 6243. Grey sandstone statuette of Vishnu on the Garuda bird. 12th century AD. 19.5 cm. From the Angkor region.

DCA 3190. Eroded sandstone torso of a 4-armed male deity. Late 11th century AD. Ca. 40 cm. From Pre Rup temple, Angkor.

DCA 4366. Dark grey sandstone head of the god Harihara with diadem and pagoda-like chignon (removed from remaining statue). Late 9th century AD. Ca. 35 cm. From Bakong temple, Roluos.

DCA 125. Smooth, dark sandstone statue of Bodhisattva Avalokitesvara with crown-like diadem and cylindrical chignon. Late 12th century AD. 81 cm. From Ta Prohm temple, Angkor.

DCA 5456. Grey sandstone female torso. Late 12th-early 13th century AD. 65 cm. From the Angkor area.

DCA 6589. Dark pink sandstone bust of a male with cylindrical chignon bearing image of Buddha. Late 10th century AD. 25 cm. From near Tap Siem, Chikreng.

DCA 5458. Grey sandstone torso of a 4-armed deity. 12th century AD. 37 cm. From the village of Sang Voeuy, Chikreng.

DCA 140. Light grey sandstone squatting male deity on a square pedestal. Late 12th century AD. 35 cm. From Ta Prohm temple. Stolen in 1993 from the Dépôt.

DCA 5684. Sandstone head of a male deity with rounded cylindrical chignon. 13th century? 27 cm. From Kompong Kdei.

DCA 751/a. Unfinished grey sandstone head of the 11-faced Buddhist god Hevajra with diadem with central medallion. Late 12th-early 13th century AD. 26 cm. From Angkor Thom, near the Gate of Death.

Local authorities complained that they had neither the resources nor the manpower to adequately police the site. Their powers only permitted them to act within Cambodia itself, which in practice meant that they could prosecute the petty thieves engaged in transporting stolen artworks to the Thai border but had no jurisdiction over the dealers who were orchestrating the trade from within Thailand. The small fry who were caught received only light sentences. The result was that by the early 1990s local peasants were being offered from $10 to $50—large sums in local terms—to remove heads from sculptures or to transport them to the frontier in oxcarts, and thefts were reportedly taking place at the rate of one a day. Artworks were even being removed to the orders of customers who had preselected them from photographs of the monuments. "I've been at a temple site where I've overheard Thai dealers discussing which pieces they're supposed to get for clients," one American conservationist claimed.

The stories from Cambodia in recent years have been so alarming that it is easy to exaggerate the extent of the problem of looting in Southeast Asia as a whole. Even at Angkor, where most freestanding works have now disappeared, the sheer size of the monumental complex serves to dilute the extent of the damage. And in the context of the entire region, whatever ravages human greed may have wrought in despoiling the archaeological legacy have been more than matched by the conservation effort; since the region's monuments were rediscovered in the 19th century, a great deal more work has gone into preserving than despoiling them. For all the setbacks, the overall record of the past two centuries has been positive.

The first attempts at conservation date back to colonial times. Borobudur led the way. The British wrested control of Java from the Dutch and controlled it for five years, from 1811 to 1816, and it was during this period that the first European visitors reached the site. Word got back to Sir Thomas Stamford Raffles, the colony's energetic governor, and he at once dispatched an army engineer to inspect and survey the ruins. The officer he chose, H. C. Cornelius, worked for six weeks with a task force of more than 200 laborers,

In a photograph taken in the 1950s, a deteriorating gallery at Angkor Wat bristles with wooden scaffolding and tripods as members of the EFEO staff reinforce and reconstruct the stones. Henri Marchal, visible at the top left of the photograph, was curator of the EFEO before World War II. He went back to Cambodia in 1947 and at the age of 71 was again appointed to head the archaeological service.

Freshly cut blocks, rough hewn and showing no attempt to duplicate the surrounding sculpture, are visible in the walls of the Bakong (right), a late-ninth-century temple complex at Angkor. Before the 1930s, conservation efforts concentrated on clearing the ruins of vegetation and reinforcing collapsing structures with concrete or wood. Henri Marchal introduced the idea of inserting new materials into the remains of the structure to stabilize and maintain the original stones.

A supervisor from the Archaeological Survey of India stands in the midst of Cambodian workers as they scrub the stones of Angkor Wat with chemicals to remove the vegetation clinging to them. As well as surface cleaning, the Indian team—who arrived in 1986—attacked the growth between stones. Scaffolding (on the tower at top left) was erected so workers could carefully dismantle the structures. The removed stones were then marked, cleaned, dried, and preserved before reassembly.

138

felling trees, removing trash, and burning brush. By the standards of the day Cornelius did his job well. Soil and other debris were left in place where necessary to buttress walls, and stone fragments were conscientiously stored close to the spots where they were found, making it easier for subsequent investigators to work out where exactly they might have come from.

Work continued in a desultory fashion after the Dutch resumed control of the island. By the late 1830s the galleries had been cleared of earth and other debris. Sadly, the excavators failed to also clear the gutters and gargoyles the original builders had installed to provide drainage. The result was that the freshly uncovered carvings were exposed to the full force of the monsoon rains without any adequate system of runoff. The impact was disastrous; sculpted reliefs were eroded, and dampness penetrated deep into the masonry.

Remedial work to unblock the rainwater channels finally went ahead in the 1870s during a fresh spate of gallery clearance. Yet the monument's condition continued to deteriorate to such an extent that an 1882 report, never acted upon, even suggested dismantling the temple and storing the reliefs in a building raised specifically to protect them from the elements.

Although the uncovering of the shrine's "hidden foot"—a first level of reliefs that was later covered over by an embankment (pages 102-103)—renewed interest in the monument in the 1880s, it was only with the turn of the century that its fortunes took a decisive turn for the better. The report of the Borobudur Commission, published in 1902, marked the start of serious conservation efforts. It recommended urgent action to shore up the most dilapidated parts of the structure—notably the corners of the galleries—and to restore the gateways, niches, and domes. Other suggestions included removing unsightly outbuildings, further improving the drainage system, and replacing the pinnacle at the summit of the shrine.

The task of carrying out the recommendations was eventually entrusted to a 33-year-old military engineer named Theodoor van Erp. He proved an inspired choice. For the first seven months of his assignment, which he took up in 1907, he concentrated on excavating the ground around the monument, unearthing a rich crop of gargoyles, lions, Buddha's heads, and other sculptures. He also tracked down carved stones that had been removed from the site to neighboring villages. Encouraged by the wealth of material he had found, he went on to win official approval for an ambitious restoration program that aimed not just to shore up what remained of the shrine but also to replace lost elements. As a result of his efforts, Borobudur was returned over the next three years to something of its original glory *(pages 150-151)*.

In the same year that Erp started work on restoring Borobudur, the monuments of Angkor were entrusted by Indochina's French rulers to the archaeologists of the École Française d'Extrême Orient (EFEO). They were to retain exclusive control of the site until 1953, the year in which Cambodia gained independence, and even after that time they continued to take the leading role, though now in collaboration with the Cambodian government. The Angkor Conservancy was set up by the school as their local headquarters.

One of EFEO's most important directors was Bernard-Philippe Groslier, the man responsible for first revealing the full extent of the Angkor complex through a series of aerial surveys con-

The success of the chemicals used by members of the Archaeological Survey of India (ASI) is evident in the photographs below. Fungus coats the gallery on the left, while an adjoining structure (below, right) stands pristine after its treatment. Frequent monitoring of the buildings' surfaces will determine the long-term effects the cleaning solutions and the painted-on sealant (right) used by the ASI will have on the temples of Angkor Wat. Iron bands and concrete buttresses put on the columns by the EFEO 60 years before, and left in place by the Indian archaeologists, still add stability to the structures.

ducted shortly after World War II. Some of the mounds revealed in the photographs have yet to be excavated, so it seems likely that Angkor still has many secrets to be uncovered. Among the most elusive is the location of the settlement area; no nearby center of population has yet been identified.

During his tenure as director of conservation at Angkor, Groslier shored up structures that seemed in danger of collapsing and tried to address the underlying problems confronting the monuments by installing a system of concealed drains. Some of the EFEO's work has been criticized as being clumsy by present-day standards—concrete pillars and struts were used to support sagging roofs, and sandstone pillars were secured with iron bands that have since rusted—but for the most part Angkor under Groslier's custodianship was a model of good conservation practice of the time.

All that was to change, however, as the shadow of the Viet-

nam War spread across the country. The security situation gradually worsened through the late 1960s and early 1970s, up to the departure of Groslier and the last maintenance crews in 1972. For seven years thereafter the monument received no official attention, and even when the Angkor Conservancy was officially restored under the directorship of Pich Keo *(pages 130-131)*, a former pupil of Groslier's, it had neither the means nor the manpower to continue his work.

By that time the task of preserving monuments in developing countries was increasingly seen as a matter of global concern, and the principal body through which conservation efforts were coordinated was the United Nations Educational, Scientific and Cultural Organization (UNESCO). Originally founded in 1945 as the United Nations' arm for worldwide intellectual cooperation, the agency established its world heritage credentials in the 1960s, with the multimillion-dollar operation to save the temples of Abu Simbel in Egypt from the rising waters of the Nile River at the time of the construction of the Aswan Dam.

As a mark of growing concern over conservation, the 1972 UNESCO General Conference promulgated the World Heritage Convention, which has subsequently turned out to be one of the organization's greatest successes; having started out with just 40 signatories, it now has over 130. It is currently the only conservation treaty of global significance embracing both cultural and natural sites.

The convention's central feature is the World Heritage List, an index of sites of global importance that now has 378 separate entries. To qualify, a location or building must first be nominated by the state in which it lies. Its claim is then evaluated by a specially appointed, nongovernmental advisory group in the light of guidelines laid down by the convention: These demand that sites should be of outstanding universal value, should meet the test of authenticity, and should be provided with legal mechanisms and a management structure sufficient to ensure long-term protection. The group's recommendations are passed on to the World Heritage Committee, which ratifies the listing.

The World Heritage List has arguably captured the public imagination to a greater extent than any of UNESCO's other initiatives. The idea it embodies, of an inventory of sites forming part of the legacy not just of one nation but of humanity as a whole, is a new

RESTORING MONUMENTS AND PRIDE

In the early 1960s, Colonel James A. Gray (U.S. Army, retd.) presented Italian officials with a plan to stabilize the renowned Leaning Tower of Pisa. The Italian government lost interest in the project before work could begin, but Gray's idea of helping countries save their architectural masterpieces lived on, and in 1965 the World Monuments Fund (WMF) was born. By 1995 the nonprofit organization's efforts had grown to more than 100 restorations in over 29 countries. "Our mandate," says executive director Bonnie Burnham, "is to preserve great archictecture and art, and convince the world that there's a collective responsibility not to let them disappear. The protection of these treasures is diminishing, while the problems are increasing."

One of the WMF's most important and far-reaching projects is the conservation of Preah Khan, a 12th-century temple complex at Angkor. In addition to structural damage, the buildings were overgrown with vegetation that had to be removed *(above, right)* before the conservation could begin.

The project, expected to take 10 years, began in 1992 with three objectives: to train young Cambodian students in fields related to conservation and restoration and to prepare these students to maintain

Angkor in the years to come; to develop a standard methodology for on-site work which can be applied to structures throughout the ancient city; and to ready this portion of Angkor for visitors.

To many Cambodians, Angkor is a symbol of their great heritage, and its restoration offers not only a sense of pride in the past but a hope for a future with new jobs and trained personnel to fill them. Officials at the WMF hope that the restoration effort at Preah Khan is a "fundamental step in the restoration of peace and prosperity to the country."

one, at least in terms of international bureaucracy. Equally innovative is the concept of mixing natural and man-made wonders in a single index, so that the Taj Mahal appears along with the Victoria Falls and the Galapagos Islands with the Statue of Liberty. At present count, 276 of the entries are classed as cultural, as against 87 natural and 15 mixed sites.

For all the list's popularity, there are limitations on what it can achieve. Sites can be registered only at the request of the state concerned, and some governments have proved more assiduous than others in putting forward candidates; while France has 20 sites inscribed and India 19, there are at present no monuments listed at all for Japan or Kenya or, in the Southeast Asian region, for Burma, Vietnam, or Laos. There is also no mechanism for monitoring the sites, despite the fact that regular checks could in the long run save money by enabling preventive measures to be taken in time to avoid the need for later, more costly repairs. In general, money for work on monuments in poorer countries is in short supply; although a World Heritage Fund has been set up, it has proved inadequate to meet all the demands made on it.

Despite these shortcomings, the list remains a useful tool in the conservation struggle, and since 1990, Borobudur, Angkor, and the Ban Chiang mound have been entered on it. In each case, inscription marked a new stage in UNESCO's involvement with the sites, though for the first two there had been an ongoing commitment that long predated the official listing.

A place on the list is, in fact, by no means a prerequisite in seeking aid from UNESCO. The organization has, for example, long been involved at Pagan, which has yet to find its way onto the register. In the wake of the 1975 earthquake, the organization was invited to provide funds and expert advisers to help with the task of reconstruction. The request was more significant in that Burma had previously proved unwilling to let foreign scholars work there.

The links forged in the wake of the disaster proved enduring. Since 1980, UNESCO has, with the help of financing from the United Nations Development Program, sponsored continuing projects devoted to surveying, restoring, and rehabilitating the Pagan monuments. One of the major areas of concern has been finding ways of bracing the buildings against the threat of future quakes, principally by inserting iron ties within the masonry.

Another has been to produce the first complete inventory of all Pagan's monuments. The idea is hardly new—in the 15th century, a Burmese king ordered all the structures to be counted, and found their number exceeded 4,000—but the sheer size of the task has deterred all previous recent attempts. The nine volumes of plans, photographs, and verbal descriptions currently in preparation will provide invaluable reference and documentation for rebuilding in case of any future catastrophe.

The work is also helping restoration teams to establish conservation priorities. A program is already under way to clean mural paintings that have been soiled by bat droppings and soot, the latter a legacy of World War II days when local people sheltering in the temples lighted cooking fires. Archaeologists have also been excavating the remains of a royal palace near the eastern gate of the ancient city. Although the wooden superstructure has long since disappeared, the dig has revealed rows of open brick cylinders, each about four feet in diameter, that are believed to have anchored wooden pillars that supported the building's roof.

D
espite Pagan's absence from the World Heritage List, the work that UNESCO is doing there fits the classic pattern of its conservation operations. The task facing the organization at Ban Chiang is very different. Although the site is unquestionably of international importance, most of its remaining treasures lie underground, buried beneath a bustling village. There is little for casual visitors to see except a site museum and one excavation trench, preserved for public viewing. Yet the pit itself is unstable, and the risks of the sides collapsing are very real. The use of impermeable sealants to shore them up can provide a temporary solution, but only increases the likelihood in the long term of a catastrophic cave-in. Small wonder, then, that the advisory group that recommended the listing of the

The exquisite murals of Pagan's Apeyadana temple are meticulously restored by Burmese workers, shown here brushing a protective preservative on the walls. In preparation for this last step, the paintings are first repaired where the original plaster has become detached, then carefully cleaned with an ammonia-based solution. Since the murals have been protected from the sun's damaging rays, once cleaned they will regain their brilliant hues.

Vandalism was motivated by religious fervor when zealots, hoping to garner favor in their faith by "improving" the sacred works of art, splashed whitewash on the walls and sculptures of this Pagan temple. Though unsightly, the stains are removable and the paintings and sculptures can be restored to their original beauty.

site described it at the time as presenting the World Heritage Committee with a challenge.

Even more is at stake at Angkor, for unless urgent action is taken to protect it, the world runs the risk of seeing one of its greatest monumental complexes hopelessly degraded. Yet the cost of merely policing its 156 square miles against looting is prohibitive, even without taking into consideration the restoration work necessary after 20 years of neglect.

Conservationists have long understood the nature of the problems confronting Angkor, at least in their broad outlines. One major area of concern is the fact that the structures rest on inadequate foundations. They were built on beds of sand that have not only failed to prevent subsidence but also permit water to penetrate the stones, a problem of saturation only partly addressed by Groslier's hidden drains.

To compound the situation, the complex's builders used the "dry masonry" method of construction, placing block upon block without the use of any kind of mortar. Bronze clamps were occasionally inserted for reinforcement, but most of these were looted centuries ago. Now only gravity holds most of the stonework in place. Perversely, the cutting back of the surrounding jungle, which at least provided shade for the monuments, has increased expansion and contraction, boosting the risk of displacement and cracking.

Other forces are also working to lever the structures apart. Tropical vegetation sprouting from cracks in the walls can be as effective as crowbars in dislodging masonry. The greatest threat comes from strangler figs, sprouting from seeds dropped by birds onto the tops of walls. The trees' roots reach down into cracks between stones, forcing them apart. Yet cutting down the trees can actually increase the danger, for the large, outer roots twining around the outside of a wall often help hold together the very structures that the smaller roots have undermined. When the tree dies and the roots rot, the risk of collapse increases.

The damage from seepage is as insidious, if less apparent. Water penetrating the fissures between the unmortared blocks becomes trapped inside the masonry. It can only escape by leaching through the stonework and eventually evaporating on the surface, where minerals in the water cause scaling. The dampness also encourages the growth of lichen, which produces acids that eat into the rock and cause further deterioration. Bat droppings, which combine with rainwater to form sulfuric acid, compound the problem even more. And the speed of vegetation growth in an area where grass can sprout three feet in a month makes constant maintenance a necessity.

Yet even after the Khmer Rouge reign of terror came to an end in 1979, political considerations prevented any effective multilateral action for more than a decade. Few countries recognized the Vietnamese-backed government of Heng Samrinh, and international assistance to the country was effectively embargoed.

One of the first countries to establish diplomatic relations with the Vietnamese-backed administration was India, and the result was that the Archaeological Survey of India (ASI) was the first foreign organization allowed to send a restoration team to the area. Arriving in 1986, the ASI team set about cutting the vegetation and cleaning the stonework of the major monuments, using techniques that had proved effective in the home country *(pages 138-141)*.

Welcome though the Indian contribution was at the time, it has since proved controversial. Critics point to the fact that one of the chemical fungicides the ASI team initially used to combat mold contained dioxin—also found in the notorious Agent Orange of the Vietnam War. Some scientists have also claimed that attempts to prevent seepage with the aid of impermeable sealants merely encouraged water to build up beneath the surface of the stone, threatening even more serious damage. Some surfaces were reportedly damaged by overzealous scrubbing by an undertrained work force.

The criticism surfaced in 1989 when UNESCO—deciding that UN-sponsored peace initiatives were sufficiently advanced to justify its involvement—sent two fact-finding missions to Angkor to investigate the state of the ruins. Round tables of experts were subsequently organized to consider the reports and to propose an action program. The work bore fruit in 1991, when a peace settlement was finally signed and the embargo on international assistance was lifted. One immediate result was that at the request of the new government Angkor was hastily installed, through an emergency procedure that bypassed several stages, on the World Heritage List.

In 1992, UNESCO opened an office in the nearby town of

TERRASSE DU ROI LEPREUX
LEPER KINGS TERRACE
RESTAURATION DE LA TERRASSE DU ROI LEPREUX
RESTORATION OF LEPER KINGS TERRACE
CHANTIER INTERDIT AU PUBLIC
NO ADMITTANCE EXCEPT ON BUSINESS
FINANCE PAR: FONDS EN DÉPOT DU GOUVERNEMENT FRANÇAIS AUPRÈS DE L'UNESCO
RÉALISATION ECOLE FRANÇAISE D'EXTRÊME-ORIENT EN COLLABORATION AVEC LA CONSERVATION D'ANGKOR
DÉBUT TRAVAUX: SEPTEMBRE 93
DURÉE: 2 ANS

French archaeologists and technicians help Cambodians conserve and restore the Terrace of the Leper King at Angkor. The effort began in 1993, picking up where the EFEO left off in 1972 when the Khmer Rouge overran Angkor. In addition to the restoration of the Terrace of the Leper King, the French government, in cooperation with UNESCO and Cambodia's Ministry of Culture, has contributed financially to training and research activities at Angkor.

Siem Reap to coordinate international conservation efforts. The following year it helped organize an intergovernmental conference in Tokyo devoted to the question of safeguarding Angkor. Finally, in 1994, the Cambodian government adopted an emergency plan based in large part on the UNESCO proposals.

The end product of this lengthy process of deliberation is an ambitious scheme for the establishment of an Angkor National Park. The plan not only encompasses restoration work on the temples and training programs for Cambodian staff, but also envisions everything from the establishment of visitor-information booths and a research institute for Angkorian studies to large-scale environmental management, including the construction of a hydroelectric dam to provide power for the region.

If Angkor's problems still seem daunting, the good news is that there is at least an encouraging precedent to suggest they can be solved. Four decades earlier, similar dangers to those threatening Angkor confronted the shrine of Borobudur. It too was built of unmortared stone on inadequate foundations. In an area where up to eight inches of rain can fall in a day in the monsoon season, water seeping through the blocks was attacking the surface reliefs. Algae and lichen disfigured the carvings. But in 1955 the Indonesian government turned to UNESCO for help, and after a lengthy effort *(pages 149-157)* Borobudur is now one of the best-preserved monuments in the world, and also one of the most popular, receiving more than one million visitors annually. The problems confronting it today are those of success. The issue of tourist pollution is already causing concern; a particular worry is that exhaust fumes from tour buses are damaging the stonework. Efforts are now under way to encourage a more environmentally friendly form of tourism, with visitors being encouraged to attend nearby workshops devoted to traditional Indonesian crafts such as batik and bamboo work.

There are many useful lessons to be learned from the Borobudur experience if Angkor is to be saved. The process of consultation and discussion currently being implemented in fact closely replicates that followed in Indonesia in the 1960s. The plan adopted by the Cambodian government for the complex's preservation is as ambitious as the Borobudur rescue—if anything more so, since it covers a much wider area and contains an environmental component more extensive in its implications than any attempted in the earlier program. Only time will tell if it will be as successful.

Meanwhile, the international community can help to preserve not just Angkor but all the world's heritage by taking effective action to shut down the illegal traffic in antiquities. Such a move implies improved policing of sales outlets and auction houses, for the looting immediately loses much of its attraction if the spoils cannot be offered on the open market. Equally important is the compilation of comprehensive registers of stolen property. Lists of this sort are already available to police forces worldwide, and measures to improve and update them are under way. The question that remains is how much of Southeast Asia's battered heritage will still be intact by the time preventive measures succeed in closing down the black-market trade at its source. Only then will the treasures of this newly dynamic region's long-forgotten empires rest secure.

THE REBIRTH OF BOROBUDUR

I n 1968 the French archaeologist Bernard-Philippe Groslier warned that the stones of the massive monument of Borobudur were about to "come down in an appalling avalanche of earth and sculptures." Constructed around AD 800 and located in central Java, the edifice had been shored up by an earlier restoration in 1911. Now, however, it was clear that the deterioration not only had continued but had accelerated to a critical point. The primary problem: Rivers of rainwater, gushing for more than 1,000 years through the unmortared stones, were washing away the hill underneath the structure. If emergency measures were not taken soon Borobudur was doomed.

To be sure, specialists in the field of conservation had heard all this before. Over the course of the previous five decades surveys had been commissioned, reports produced, plans made, and then, owing to various conditions—including worldwide depression, war, and lack of funds—the badly needed reconstruction had nev-

er been started. What gave weight to Groslier's dire prediction was that he was conducting his survey of Borobudur on behalf of UNESCO (United Nations Educational, Scientific, and Cultural Organization), the organization that had, just two years before, rescued the temple of the Egyptian pharaoh Ramses II at Abu Simbel from destruction by flooding created during the construction of the Aswan Dam on the Nile. In partnership with UNESCO, Indonesia could now begin the job of rescuing Borobudur.

With financial help from countries throughout the world, the project was launched in 1973. Soon the area around the monument was transformed into a construction site as equipment and personnel moved in to begin work. Giant cranes (*above*) were put in place to help remove and replace thousands of stones and statues while temporary facilities were built to house the various conservation efforts. The story of the rebirth of Borobudur is told on the following pages.

A DUTCH ENGINEER SAVES THE DAY

By 1900 the once-majestic Borobudur resembled a pile of stones *(below)*. The extent of the deterioration galvanized the Dutch colonial government into action, and in 1907, Theodoor van Erp, a young officer serving in the Royal Engineers, took on the task of conservation. The work of the Dutch team was extraordinary in its scope and, because of Erp's single-minded focus on what he considered to be the principles of good restoration, the project became a model of conservation for the times. A cautious engineer and talented artist, Erp had great respect for the monument, which helped him resist the urge to add fanciful reconstructions and keep the work as faithful as possible to what he believed was the building's original character.

By 1911 the work was complete. Spouts were repaired to divert water from the interior of the monument; reliefs, balustrades, stairs, and ornamental niches of the lower levels were renovated; and the three upper terraces were rebuilt. A lasting contribution of Erp's work, however, was not related to engineering. He recommended that a photographic record be made of the monument during all phases of the restoration. This would prove to be an important tool in monitoring the deterioration of Borobudur in the decades to follow.

One of the earliest images of Borobudur, this daguerreotype (above) *was taken around 1850 and shows the tilted galleries of the first level. Though unable to correct the tilt, Erp stabilized the lower levels by adding concrete to the floors.*

Erp (above) *stands among the stupas of Borobudur before restoration. The bell-shaped structures, some of which had been looted of their statues before 1900, were in desperate need of repair. Although every effort was made to use only original materials in the* rebuilding of the circular terraces, so many pieces of the stupas were missing that more than 50 percent of each of the 72 structures had to be built from new stone. The photos below, taken before and after the restoration, show the magnitude of the job.

A GLOBAL PARTNERSHIP IS FORMED

Taking 10 years to complete and with a final cost of more than $25 million, the most recent effort to restore Borobudur was complex and, over the life of the project, would employ as many as 600 people. UNESCO and Indonesia called upon specialists in the fields of architecture, archaeology, engineering, soil mechanics, seismology, conservation techniques, hydrology, and geology to devise a plan of attack—a long-range program to guide and organize the massive project.

Acting on the recommendation of a restoration committee, the project's organizers proposed a three-part plan: insert a drainage system to keep rainwater from the monument's core; stabilize the building by installing concrete slabs under the terraces; and finally,

conserve the stone blocks, statues, and reliefs that make up the structure.

In order to accomplish these goals, workers first removed more than one million stones from the lower five terraces. Because Erp's 1907-1911 reconstruction of the upper portion containing the 72 bell-shaped stupas was still sound, the stupas were left in place. While the stones were going through conservation, reinforced concrete slabs were poured to stabilize the structure, and a new drainage system was installed to protect the monument from water damage. When that portion of the plan was completed, the treated stones and statues were returned to their original positions, this time on a well-drained, secure platform.

Buddhas, identified with chalk numbers on their backs, await removal from the terraces of Borobudur. Each statue and stone was tagged, the number logged into a computer-run tracking system, then removed to a separate building for treatment.

Workmen (above) *pile numbered blocks onto specially designed pallets while cranes wait at the base of the structure (below) to lift and carry them away. Since no mortar was used in the construction of Borobudur, each stone was cut to fit the one next* to it; *in order to keep the structure stable, each stone had to be returned to its original position. A modern stone mason (above, right) using ancient techniques, carefully chisels the volcanic stones, which are then installed in the new drainage system.*

BEAUTY TREATMENTS FOR BUDDHA

The reliefs and statues that decorate Borobudur offer visitors a magnificent collection of ancient Buddhist art. Unfortunately, they also offer a home for destructive parasitic organisms, often called stone cancers. Because of the high level of humidity in the region, some of the water that flows through the structure is retained inside the porous volcanic rock. The moist stones provide a perfect home for mosses, algae, and lichens to grow and attack the delicate carvings and accelerate the process of disintegration. A related problem is the water that is forced to the surface of the rock. As the water evaporates, minerals left on the surface of the stone form brilliant white blemishes.

Experts studied these problems and a plan of conservation took shape. As they were removed from the monument, stones needing treatment were housed in buildings protected from the elements. Their surfaces were cleaned with a dry brush and, in some cases, water. If the discoloration or infestation was stubborn, a mild chemical solution was applied. The wet stones were then dried, mechanically if necessary, and treated with a herbicide before replacement.

There is evidence suggesting that when it was first built, Borobudur was covered with plaster, its decorations brightly painted. While the restorers lacked documentation to duplicate that original appearance, visitors are now able to view the carvings and statues in all their original beauty.

Buddhas awaiting preservation become handy hooks for the workers' clothes. The heads of Buddhas from Borobudur, once prized as collector's items, were sometimes taken by thieves and sold to private collectors.

A conservation worker carefully paints a chemical "face pack" made of clay and chemicals on a statue of Buddha. Many of the Indonesians who were trained at Borobudur by UNESCO are now a part of the permanent staff working to preserve and maintain the monument.

Heavy equipment, like the crane in the photograph below, was needed to move the enormous stones and life-size statues of Borobudur. After the restoration, construction materials and structures were removed and an archaeological park was built.

Tourists, who number more than one million annually, clamber over the restored terraces of Borobudur. The Indonesian government monitors the site to ensure against further deterioration from the elements and to provide effective security measures to deter vandals. The ongoing challenge for Indonesia is to make Borobudur available to all of its citizens while guaranteeing the monument's continued conservation.

THE FLOWERING OF SOUTHEAST ASIA

A crossroads between India and China, Southeast Asia has long been considered a repository of the cultures of its two great neighbors. The influence of China and, especially, India have indeed been great. Representations of the Hindu demon Kala, for example *(below)*, are more numerous on temples there than in India itself. But recent study has shown that the civilizations that thrived in this part of the world were no mere transplants: They had been developing their own ways since prehistoric times.

About 10,000 years ago, at the end of the last Ice Age, rising sea levels flooded the coastal areas of Southeast Asia: The landmass shrank, and the territory that once connected Indonesia to the mainland disappeared. All across the region peoples using a stone technology known as Hoabinhian emerged, exploiting the food sources of the new coastlines and river estuaries and the dense vegetation of the interior. Plant remains from the Spirit Cave in northwestern Thailand, an important Stone Age site, indicate what might be the earliest evidence of cultivation in Southeast Asia.

PREHISTORIC
8000 BC—AD 100

DONG SON DRUM

The adoption of farming was a gradual process. As communities increased in size, they began to exploit the resource of wild rice and then to farm the crop, at first along streams and then in submerged paddy fields. Using elaborate irrigation schemes, such wet-rice farming—ideally suited to monsoon Asia—could produce up to three crops a year of what was to become the region's staple food. Rice cultivation was labor intensive, however, requiring the construction of dikes and canals to channel and retain the water; the settlement of drier areas may have led to the development of larger, more organized settlements.

Many rice-farming communities of the mainland had access to tin and copper. Around 2000 BC the peoples of the Ban Chiang cultural tradition in northeastern Thailand—and perhaps elsewhere in the region—alloyed these metals to produce bronze tools and ornaments. Around 700 BC ironworking developed as well, and during the last centuries before the modern era metallurgy spread to the islands of Southeast Asia. Trade with the islands is revealed by the widespread distribution of ceremonial bronze drums *(above)* named after the site of Dong Son in Vietnam. By the end of the millennium, Malay seafarers had even established commercial links as far away as the East African coast.

PROTOHISTORIC
AD 100—AD 800

THAI VISHNU

HISTORIC
AD 800—AD 1400

ANGKOR THOM GATE

The first centuries after Christ marked a period of major change for Southeast Asia. Jutting out from the Asian continent to separate the Bay of Bengal and the South China Sea, the peninsula stood between the two great cultures of India and China. Along its coasts Indian traders in search of gold, spices, and other valuables began to establish settlements. With the traders came their religions—Buddhism and Hinduism—and their gods, such as Shiva, the creator, and Vishnu, the preserver *(above)*. They also brought writing, the use of coins, and concepts of state and kingship that would have a profound impact on the civilizations of Southeast Asia.

From small principalities like Funan, which dominated the Mekong Delta during the first half of the millennium, these Indian ideas began to permeate the region. They spread north to the land of Zhenla, eventual successor to Funan; northwest to Thailand and Burma; and to Vietnam's central and southern coasts. By AD 600 the religions and many of the cultural attributes of the subcontinent had taken firm root throughout the mainland and the islands of Southeast Asia. Blending Indian and local ways, new civilizations began to form. During the historic period, these so-called Indianized kingdoms would flourish and bring forth a golden age.

The years AD 800 to 1000 were a time of monumental architecture in Southeast Asia, when Hindu and Buddhist stone temples were built at a rate matched only by the growth of new kingdoms. These *mandalas*—or states—were made up of fluctuating tracts of territory centered in the court of a dominant overlord, whose status attracted supporters and made possible the exercise of power. An overlord could enhance his status by associating himself with the gods of India.

The most famous of these *mandalas* was that of the Khmer, which covered most of modern Cambodia. The Khmer rulers filled their capital of Angkor with religious monuments, such as those in Angkor Thom, the gate for which is shown above. Northwest of Angkor lay the kingdoms of Thailand, and beyond, the Burmese empire of Pagan. Along the South China Sea were the territories of the Annamites and the Chams, and on the Indonesian island of Java, kingdoms near Borobudur.

The mainland states were at their height from the 11th to 13th centuries. But this era also saw the rise of new powers. In 1259 the Mongols invaded Annam and by century's end overran Pagan. The Thais of China's Yunnan province moved south into what is now Thailand, and in the 15th century, they sacked Angkor. The classical era of Southeast Asian history was over.

ACKNOWLEDGMENTS

The editors wish to thank the following individuals and institutions for their valuable assistance in the preparation of this volume:

Roberto Ciarla, Museo Nazionale d'Arte Orientale, Rome; Russell Ciochon, University of Iowa, Iowa City, Iowa; Ben Finney, University of Hawaii, Honolulu; Inez Forbes, United Nations Educational, Scientific, and Cultural Organization (UNESCO), Paris; Tilman Frasch, Südasien Institut, Universitat Heidelberg, Germany; Carlo Giantomassi, Rome; Madeleine Giteau, Paris; Ha Van Tan, Social Sciences Research Institute, Hanoi; Charles Higham, University of Otago, Dunedin, New Zealand; Jamie James, New York; Susanne Knödel, Hamburgisches Museum für Völkerkunde, Germany; Elisabeth Kraemer-Singh, Bonn; Albert Le Bonheur, Conservateur en Chef au Musée Guimet, Paris; Elizabeth Moore, School of Oriental and African Studies, London; Hideo Noguchi, The Physical Culture Heritage, UNESCO, Paris; Eve Nolan, National Geographic Image Collection, Washington, D.C.; William Schauffler, Annapolis, Md.; Tina Shaffer, Bishop Museum, Honolulu; Vu The Long, Institute of Archaeology, Hanoi; Guo Weifu, Cultural Relics Publishing House, Beijing; Donatella Zari, Rome.

PICTURE CREDITS

BIBLIOGRAPHY

BOOKS

Adams, Roy. *Borobudur: In Photographs—Past and Present*. Leiden: University of Leiden, 1990.

Allen, Oliver E., and the Editors of Time-Life Books. *The Pacific Navigators* (The Seafarers series). Alexandria, Virginia: Time-Life Books, 1980.

Barabudur: History and Significance of a Buddhist Monument (Berkeley Buddist series). Berkeley: The Regents of the University of California, 1981.

Barbier, Jean Paul, and Douglas Newton, eds. *Islands and Ancestors: Indigenous Styles of Southeast Asia*. New York: The Metropolitan Museum of Art, 1988.

Bellwood, Peter S. *Prehistory of the Indo-Malaysian Archipelago*. Sydney: Academic Press Australia, 1985.

Bernard, Bruce. *Photodiscovery: Masterworks of Photography 1840-1940*. New York: Harry N. Abrams, 1980.

Beurdeley, Cécile. *Sur les Routes de la Soie*. Fribourg: Office du Livre S. A., 1985.

Boisselier, Jean. *Trends in Khmer Art*. Ed. by Natasha Eilenberg and trans. by Natasha Eilenberg and Melvin Elliott. Ithaca, New York: Southeast

Asia Program, Cornell University, 1989.

Bologna, Gianfranco. *Guide to Birds of the World*. Ed. by John L. Bull. New York: Simon and Schuster, 1988.

Borobudur: Beauty in Peril. Paris: United Nations Educational, Scientific, and Cultural Organization, 1973.

Bosch, F. D. K. *Selected Studies in Indonesian Archaeology*. The Hague: Martinus Nijhoff, 1961.

Carter, Michael. *Archaeology*. Poole, England: Blandford Press, 1980.

The Chinese Bronzes of Yunnan. London: Sidgwick and Jackson, 1983.

Ciochon, Russell, John W. Olsen, and Jamie James. *Other Origins: The Search for the Giant Ape in Human Prehistory*. New York: Bantam Books, 1990.

Coedès, Georges. *The Making of South East Asia*. Trans. by H. M. Wright. Berkeley: University of California Press, 1967.

Colani, Madeleine. *Mégalithes du Haut-Laos*, Vol. 1. Paris: Les Éditions d'Art et d'Histoire, 1935.

Color, Rev. ed. (LIFE Library of Photography series). Alexandria, Virginia: Time-Life Books, 1981.

Colton, Joel G., and the Editors of Time-Life Books. *Twentieth Century*

(Great Ages of Man series). New York: Time-Life Books, 1968.

Dagens, Bruno. *Angkor: Heart of an Asian Empire*. New York: Harry N. Abrams, 1995.

Dagens, Bruno, and Claude Jacques. *One Hundred Missing Objects*. Paris: International Council of Museums and EFEO, 1993.

Delpar, Helen, ed. *The Discoverers: An Encyclopedia of Explorers and Exploration*. New York: McGraw-Hill, 1980.

Documentary Photography, Rev. ed. (LIFE Library of Photography series). Alexandria, Virginia: Time-Life Books, 1983.

Dumarcay, Jacques. *Borobudur*. Trans. and ed. by Michael Smithies. Singapore: Oxford University Press, 1991.

Edmonds, I. G. *The Khmers of Cambodia: The Story of a Mysterious People*. Indianapolis: The Bobbs-Merrill Company, 1970.

Finney, Ben. *Voyage of Rediscovery: A Cultural Odyssey through Polynesia*. Berkeley: The Regents of the University of California, 1994.

Fontein, Jan. *The Sculpture of Indonesia*. Washington, D.C.: National Gallery of Art, 1990.

Freeman, Michael, and Roger Warner.

Angkor: The Hidden Glories. Boston: Houghton Mifflin, 1990.

Fujiwara, Hiroshi. *Khmer Ceramics from the Kamratan Collection in the Southeast Asian Ceramics Museum, Kyoto.* New York: Oxford University Press, 1990.

Guy, John. *Ceramic Traditions of South-East Asia* (The Asia Collection series). New York: Oxford University Press, 1989.

Hasson, Haskia. *Ancient Buddhist Art from Burma.* Singapore: Taisei Gallery, 1993.

Hedgecoe, John. *The Photographer's Handbook.* New York: Alfred A. Knopf, 1982.

Hersey, Irwin. *Indonesian Primitive Art.* Singapore: Oxford University Press, 1991.

Higham, Charles. *The Archaeology of Mainland Southeast Asia: From 10,000 B.C. to the Fall of Angkor.* Cambridge: Cambridge University Press, 1989.

Higham, Charles, and Rachanie Thorsat. *Khok Phandom Di: Prehistoric Adaptation to the World's Richest Habitat.* Fort Worth: Harcourt Brace College Publishers, 1994.

Holt, Claire. *Art in Indonesia: Continuities and Change.* Ithaca, New York: Cornell University Press, 1967.

Htin, Aung Maung. *A History of Burma.* New York: Columbia University Press, 1967.

Ishizawa, Yoshiaki, and Yasushi Kono, eds. *Study and Preservation of Historic Cities of Southeast Asia.* Tokyo: The Institute of Asian Cultures, Sophia University, 1986.

Janse, Olov R. T.:
Archaeological Research in Indo-China, Vols. 1 and 2. Cambridge: Harvard University Press, 1947 and 1951.
Archaeological Research in Indo-China, Vol. 3. Bruges, Belgium: St. Catherine Press, 1958.

Kempers, A. J. Bernet. *Ageless Borobudur.* Arnhem, The Netherlands: Servire Wassenaar, 1976.

Klein, Wilhelm. *Burma* (Insight Guides series). Singapore: APA Productions, 1986.

Kossak, Steven. *The Arts of South and Southeast Asia.* New York: The Metropolitan Museum of Art, 1994.

Krom, Nicolaas J. *Barabudur: Archaeological Description.* The Hague: Martinus Nijhoff, 1927.

Leonowens, Anna Harriette. *The English Governess at the Siamese Court: Being Recollections of Six Years in the Royal Palace at Bangkok.* Boston: Fiels, Osgood, 1870.

Lerner, Martin. *The Flame and the Lotus: Indian and Southeast Asian Art from the Kronos Collection.* New York: The Metropolitan Museum of Art, 1984.

Light and Film, Rev. ed. (LIFE Library of Photography series). Alexandria, Virginia: Time-Life Books, 1981.

Luce, G. H. *Phases of Pre-Pagán Burma: Languages and History,* Vol. 1. New York: Oxford University Press, 1985.

Lueras, Leonard. *Bali: The Ultimate Island.* Singapore: Times Editions, 1987.

Lutz, Albert. *Dian: Ein versunkenes Königreich in China.* Zürich: Museum Rietberg Zürich, 1986.

McIntosh, Jane. *The Practical Archaeologist: How We Know What We Know about the Past.* New York: Facts on File, 1986.

Madsen, Axel. *Silk Roads: The Asian Adventures of Clara and André Malraux.* New York: Pharos Books, 1989.

Malleret, Louis. *L'Archéologie du Delta du Mékong,* Vol. 1. Paris: École Française d'Extrême-Orient, 1959.

Marr, David G., and A. C. Milner, eds. *Southeast Asia in the 9th to 14th Centuries.* Singapore: Institute of Southeast Asian Studies, 1986.

Mattera-Corneloup, Marie. *Le Cambodge: Années Vingt.* Paris: Musée Albert Kahn, 1992.

Mazzeo, Donatella, and Chiara Silviantonini. *Monuments of Civilization: Ancient Cambodia.* New York: Grosset & Dunlap, 1978.

Miksic, John N.:
Borobudur: Golden Tales of the Buddhas. Boston: Shambhala, 1990.
Old Javanese Gold. Singapore: Ideation, 1990.

Moore, Elizabeth H. *Moated Sites in Early North East Thailand.* Oxford: B.A.R., 1988.

Narasimhaiah, B. *Angkor Vat: India's Contribution in Conservation 1986-1993.* New Delhi: Archaeological Survey of India, Government of India, 1994.

Pal, Pratapaditya. *The Sensuous Immortals: A Selection of Sculptures from the Pan-Asian Collection.* Los Angeles: Los Angeles County Museum of Art, 1977.

Pal, Pratapaditya, ed. *Asian Art: Selections from the Norton Simon Museum.* Pasadena, California: Norton Simon Museum, 1988.

Pichard, Pierre. *Inventory of Monuments at Pagan,* Vol. 1. Paris: UNESCO, 1992.

Pigott, Vincent C., and Surapol Natapintu. "Archaeological Investigations into Prehistoric Copper Production: The Thailand Archaeometallurgy Project 1984-1986." In *The Beginning of the Use of Metals and Alloys,* ed. by Robert Maddin. Cambridge: MIT Press, 1988.

Pirazzoli-t'Serstevens, Michèle. *The Han Dynasty.* Trans. by Janet Seligman. New York: Rizzoli, 1982.

Provencher, Ronald. *Mainland Southeast Asia: An Anthropological Perspective.* Pacific Palisades, California: Goodyear Publishing Company, 1975.

Pym, Christopher. *The Ancient Civilization of Angkor.* New York: The New American Library, 1968.

Pym, Christopher, ed. *Henri Mouhot's Diary.* London: Oxford University Press, 1966.

Rainey, Froelich. *Reflections of a Digger: Fifty Years of World Archaeology.* Philadelphia: The University Museum of Archaeology and Anthropology, University of Pennsylvania, 1992.

Rawson, Philip. *The Art of Southeast Asia.* New York: Frederick A. Praeger, 1967.

Reed, Charles A., ed. *World Anthropology: Origins of Agriculture.* The Hague: Mouton Publishers, 1977.

Riboud, Marc. *Angkor: The Serenity of Buddhism.* London: Thames and Hudson, 1993.

Rooney, Dawn. *Khmer Ceramics.* New York: Oxford University Press, 1984.

Rosati, Gloria, and Francesco Buranelli. *Vatican Museums: Egyptians and Etruscans.* Trans. by Martha King. Florence: SCALA, 1983.

Sauer, Carl O. *Agricultural Origins and Dispersals* (Bowman Memorial Lectures series). New York: The American Geographical Society, 1952.

162

Scheltema, Johann F. *Monumental Java.* New Delhi: Asian Educational Services, 1985.

Scheurleer, Pauline Lunsingh, and Marijke J. Klokke. *Ancient Indonesian Bronzes.* Leiden, The Netherlands: E. J. Brill, 1988.

Siribhadra, Smitthi, and Elizabeth Moore. *Palaces of the Gods: Khmer Art and Architecture in Thailand.* Ed. by Narisa Chakra. Bangkok: River Books, 1992.

Smith, Bruce D. *The Emergence of Agriculture.* New York: Scientific American Library, 1995.

Smith, R. B., and W. Watson, eds. *Early South East Asia.* New York: Oxford University Press, 1979.

Soebadio, Haryati, ed. *Art of Indonesia.* Trans. by John Miksic. Singapore: Editions Didier Millet, 1992.

Soekmono, Dr. *Chandi Borobudur: A Monument of Mankind.* Paris: UNESCO, 1976.

Splendors of the Past (Lost Cities of the Ancient World series). Washington, D.C.: The National Geographic Society, 1981.

Stargardt, Janice. *The Ancient Pyu of Burma,* Vol. 1. Cambridge: University of Cambridge, England, PACSEA, 1990.

Strachan, Paul. *Pagan: Art and Architecture of Old Burma.* Arran, Scotland: Kiscadale Publications, 1989.

Tarling, Nicholas, ed. *The Cambridge History of Southeast Asia,* Vol. 1. Cambridge: Cambridge University Press, 1992.

Taylor, Keith Weller. *The Birth of Vietnam.* Berkeley: University of California Press, 1983.

Taylor, Paul Michael, and Lorraine V. Aragon. *Beyond the Java Sea: Art of Indonesia's Outer Islands.* Washington, D.C.: Smithsonian Institution, 1991.

Thaw, Aung. *The Excavations at Beikthano.* Rangoon: Ministry of Union Culture, 1968.

Thwin, Aung Michael. *Pagan: The Origins of Modern Burma.* Honolulu: University of Hawaii Press, 1985.

Treasures from the National Museum: Bangkok. Bangkok: The National Museum Volunteers, 1987.

Van Beek, Steve, and Luca Invernizzi Tettoni. *The Arts of Thailand.* New York: Thames and Hudson, 1991.

van de Velde, Pieter, ed. *Prehistoric Indonesia: A Reader.* The Netherlands: Foris Publications, 1984.

van Leur, J. C. *Indonesian Trade and Society.* The Hague: W. van Hoeve, 1955.

White, Joyce C.:
Ban Chiang: Discovery of a Lost Bronze Age. Philadelphia: The University Museum, University of Pennsylvania, 1982.
"Early East Asian Metallurgy: The Southern Tradition." In *The Beginning of the Use of Metals and Alloys,* ed. by Robert Maddin. Cambridge: MIT Press, 1988.

Wolters, O. W. *History, Culture, and Region in Southeast Asian Perspectives.* Singapore: Institute of Southeast Asian Studies, 1982.

The World Atlas of Archaeology. London: Mitchell Beazley, 1988.

Zhou Daguan. *The Customs of Cambodia.* Bangkok: Siam Society, 1992.

PERIODICALS

Asian Perspectives: A Journal of Archaeology and Prehistory of Asia, Vols. 9, 13, 25, 1966—.

Batcheller, Jill. "The Path to the Past May Be the Road to Mandalay." *Liberal Arts,* University of Iowa, Winter 1995.

Bayard, D., and Charoenwongsa, P. "Chet Gorman: An Appreciation." *Asian Perspectives,* April 25, 1982.

Bingham, Robert. "Political Ruins." *The New Yorker,* October 18, 1993.

Bökemeier, Rolf. "Auf Bruch am Mekong." *Geo,* January 1994.

Cameron, Christina. "The Strengths and Weaknesses of the World Heritage Convention." *Nature & Resources,* Vol. 28, No. 3, 1992.

Ciochon, Russell L.:
"The Ape That Was." *Natural History,* November 1991.
"Jungle Monuments of Angkor." *Natural History,* January 1990.

Ciochon, Russell L., and Jamie James:
"The Battle of Angkor Wat." *New Scientist,* October 14, 1989.
"The Glory That Was Ankor." *Archaeology,* March/April 1994.
"The Power of Pagan." *Archaeology,* September/October 1992.
"Travel: Land of Cham." *Archaeology,* May/June 1992.

Dickenson, Doris. "The Rape of Ban Chiang." *The Asia Magazine,* June 2, 1974.

Eisenberg, Jerome M. "The Pillage of Angkor." *Minerva,* March/April 1994.

Expedition (Special issue: Ban Chiang), Summer 1982.

Garrett, W. E.:
"Pagan: On the Road to Mandalay." *National Geographic,* March 1971.
"The Temples of Angkor: Will They Survive?" *National Geographic,* May 1982.

Gorman, Chester F.:
"The Hoabinhian and After: Subsistence Patterns in Southeast Asia during the Late Pleistocene and Early Recent Periods." *World Archaeology,* February 1971.
"The Pillaging of Ban Chiang." *Art Research News,* Vol. 1, 1981.

Gorman, Chester, and Pisit Charoenwongsa. "Ban Chiang: A Mosaic of Impressions from the First Two Years." *Expedition,* Summer 1976.

Harker, Carol. "Fleshing Out Old Bones." *Iowa Alumni Review,* May 1991.

Higham, Charles, and Rachanie Thosarat. "Thailand's Good Mound." *Natural History,* December 1994.

Jokilehto, Jukka. "Training and Restoration Programmes for Cultural Heritage." *Nature & Resources,* Vol. 28, No. 3, 1992.

"The Lands and Peoples of Southeast Asia." *National Geographic,* March 1971.

Morton, W. Brown, III. "Indonesia Rescues Ancient Borobudur." *National Geographic,* January 1983.

Pigott, V. C. "Pre-Industrial Mineral Exploitation and Metal Production in Thailand." *MASCA Journal,* 1986.

Prott, Lyndel V. "From Admonition to Action: UNESCO's Role in the Protection of Cultural Heritage." *Nature & Resources,* Vol. 28, No. 3, 1992.

Rossion, Pierre. "Mystérieuse Plaine des Jarres au Laos." *Archeologia/Sommaire,* May 1992.

Scheurleer, Pauline Lunsingh. "Ancient Gold Jewellery from Central Java." *Arts of Asia,* July/August 1994.

Shenon, Philip. "Washing Buddha's Face." *The New York Times Magazine,* June 21, 1992.

Soekmono, R. "Indonesia's Buddhist Sanctuary: A Sermon in Stone." *The UNESCO Courier,* February 1983.

Solheim, Wilhelm G.:
"A Brief History of the Dongson Concept." *Asian Perspectives,* Vol. 28, No. 1, 1990.
"New Light on a Forgotten Past." *National Geographic,* March 1971.

Stovel, Herb. "The Evaluation of Cultural Properties for the World Heritage List." *Nature & Resources,* Vol. 28, No. 3, 1992.

Valicenti, Trish. "Return to Angkor." *Gamma Magazine,* April 1994.

Warner, Roger:
"Good News from Angkor Wat." *Geo,* May 1982.
"In Angkor, A Glimmer of Hope among the Ruins." *Smithsonian,* May 1990.

Whitbread, K. J. "Mediaeval Burmese Wall-Paintings from a Temple at Pagan Now in the Hamburgisches Museum für Völkerkunde, Hamburg." *Oriens Extremus,* Vol. 18. Wiesbaden, Hamburg, 1971.

White, Peter T.:
"Ancient Glory in Stone." *National Geographic,* May 1982.
"Laos Today." *National Geographic,* June 1987.
"Mosaic of Cultures." *National Geographic,* March 1971.

Yarrow, Andrew L. "Private Group Leading Angkor Restoration." *New York Times,* December 25, 1991.

OTHER SOURCES
"Art and Archeology of Viet Nam: Asian Crossroad of Cultures." Exhibition Guide. Smithsonian Institution, 1961.

"The Art and Monuments of Java." Pamphlet. *The Unesco Courier,* June 1968.

Bayard, Donn, ed. "Southeast Asian Archaeology at the XV Pacific Science Congress." Papers presented in Symposium K.1.e: "The Origins of Agriculture, Metallurgy, and the State in Mainland Southeast Asia." Dunedin, New Zealand, February 8-10, 1983.

"Borobudur: Beauty in Peril." Pamphlet. Paris: UNESCO, 1973.

"The Conquest of Time." Pamphlet. Paris: UNESCO, 1983.

"Eternal Beauty: Jewelry of Old Javanese Gold 4th—15th Century." Trans. by Nicoline Gatehouse. Royal Tropical Institute, 1993.

Finney, Ben. "Colonizing an Island World." University of Hawaii: Unpublished manuscript.

Glover, I.C. "Early Trade between Indian and Southeast Asia: A Link in the Development of a World Trading System." Occasional Paper No. 16. England: Centre for South-East Asian Studies, The University of Hull, 1989.

Glover, Ian, ed. "Southeast Asian Archaeology 1990." Conference proceedings. United Kingdom: The University of Hull.

Glover, Ian, and Emily Glover, eds. "Southeast Asian Archaeology 1986." Conference proceedings. University College London: Institute of Archaeology, September 1986.

Ishizawa, Y., ed., et al. "La Renaissance Culturelle du Cambodge (2)." Report. Sophia University, 1990.

Kal, W. H., ed. "Old Javanese Gold (4th—15th Century): An Archaeometrical Approach." Bulletin No. 334. Royal Tropical Institute, 1994.

Kossak, Steven. "The Arts of South and Southeast Asia." The Metropolitan Museum of Art, 1994.

Loofs-Wissowa, H. H. E., ed. "The Diffusion of Material Culture." 28th International Congress of Orientalists. Seminar proceedings. University of Hawaii, 1971.

"Pelita Borobudur." Reports and Documents of the Consultative Committee for the Safeguarding of Borobudur. Vol. 1, 10, 11, 1982.

"Safeguarding and Development of Angkor." 1993.

"UNESCO in Cambodia 1951-1993." Report. The Inter-Governmental Conference on the Safeguarding and Development of the Historical Area of Angkor. October 1993.

"Water Management in the Angkor Area." Report. Angkor Foundation, Budapest, Hungary. June 1993.

World Monuments Fund:
"Preah Khan Conservation Project: Historic City of Angkor." Report V. July 1994.
"Saving Our Past: A Race against Time—1965-1990." Catalogue, 1990.
"World Monuments Fund in Cambodia." Angkor Field Reports. Pamphlet.

INDEX

CHINA

Yangzi R

BAN CHIANG POT

ANANDA TEMPLE AT PAGAN

INDIA

Irrawaddy River

Salween River

Mekong River

Red River

Dian

Co Loa

Hanoi

•Pagan

•Beikthano

Hoa Binh

•Sri Ksetra

Spirit Cave

Dong Son

Lang Trang Caves

Phu Lon

Thaton

Non Nok Tha

Ban Chiang

Mi Son

BAY OF BENGAL

Rangoon

Sukhothai

Dong Duong

Ongbah Cave

Khok Phanom Di

Angkor •

Tonle Sap

JAYAVARMAN VII

SRI LANKA

Phonm Penh

Oc Eo

SOUTH

N

Singapore

SUMATRA

INDIAN OCEAN

JAVA

Borobudu

Prambanan